ITALY
in Pictures

Alison Behnke

Lerner Publications Company

Contents

Lerner Publishing Group realizes that current information and statistics quickly become out of date. To extend the usefulness of the Visual Geography Series, we developed www.vgsbooks.com, a website offering links to up-to-date information, as well as in-depth material, on a wide variety of subjects. All of the websites listed on www.vgsbooks.com have been carefully selected by researchers at Lerner Publishing Group. However, Lerner Publishing Group is not responsible for the accuracy or suitability of the material on any website other than <www.lernerbooks.com>. It is recommended that students using the Internet be supervised by a parent or teacher. Links on www.vgsbooks.com will be regularly reviewed and updated as needed.

Copyright © 2003 by Lerner Publications Company

All rights reserved. International copyright secured. No part of this book may be reproduced, stored in a retrieval system, or transmitted in any form or by any means— electronic, mechanical, photocopying, recording, or otherwise—without the prior written permission of Lerner Publications Company, except for the inclusion of brief quotations in an acknowledged review.

Lerner Publications Company
A division of Lerner Publishing Group
241 First Avenue North
Minneapolis, MN 55401 U.S.A.

Website address: www.lernerbooks.com

web enhanced @ www.vgsbooks.com

Library of Congress Cataloging-in-Publication Data

Behnke, Alison.
    Italy in pictures / by Alison Behnke.—Rev. & expanded.
        p.   cm. — (Visual geography series)
    Includes bibliographical references and index.
    Summary: A historical and current look at Italy, discussing the land, the government, the people, and
the economy.
    ISBN: 0-8225-0368-9 (lib. bdg. : alk. paper)
    1. Italy—Pictorial works—Juvenile literature. 2. Italy—Juvenile literature. [1. Italy.] I. Title. II. Visual
geography series (Minneapolis, Minn.)
DG420 .B44 2003
914.5—dc21   2001005483

Manufactured in the United States of America
1 2 3 4 5 6 - JR - 08 07 06 05 04 03

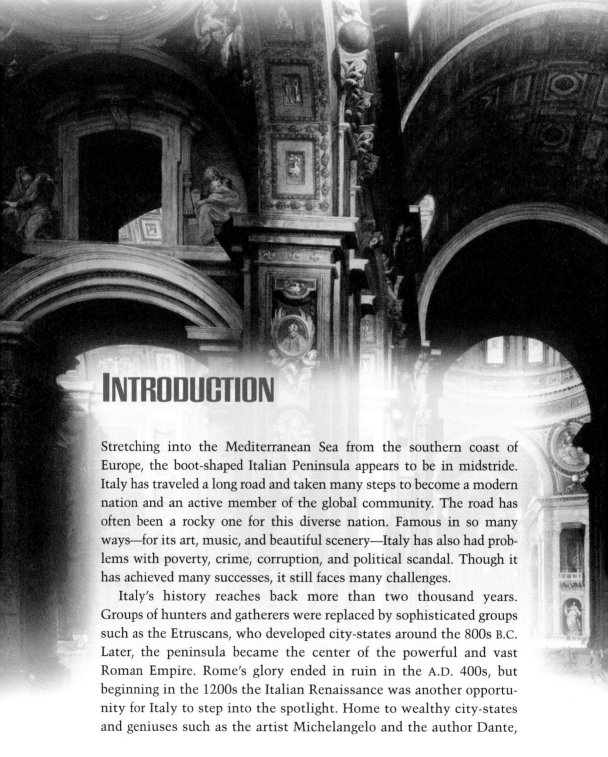

INTRODUCTION

Stretching into the Mediterranean Sea from the southern coast of Europe, the boot-shaped Italian Peninsula appears to be in midstride. Italy has traveled a long road and taken many steps to become a modern nation and an active member of the global community. The road has often been a rocky one for this diverse nation. Famous in so many ways—for its art, music, and beautiful scenery—Italy has also had problems with poverty, crime, corruption, and political scandal. Though it has achieved many successes, it still faces many challenges.

Italy's history reaches back more than two thousand years. Groups of hunters and gatherers were replaced by sophisticated groups such as the Etruscans, who developed city-states around the 800s B.C. Later, the peninsula became the center of the powerful and vast Roman Empire. Rome's glory ended in ruin in the A.D. 400s, but beginning in the 1200s the Italian Renaissance was another opportunity for Italy to step into the spotlight. Home to wealthy city-states and geniuses such as the artist Michelangelo and the author Dante, the nation continued to build on its already rich cultural heritage. However, the city-states constantly fought among themselves, and the country fell to domination by Spain, Austria, and France.

This outside rule continued until 1861, when Italy was unified as the Kingdom of Italy. The new nation, like much of the rest of Europe, fought in World War I (1914–1918) and in World War II (1939–1945). Invaded during the second global conflict, and the scene of devastating battles, Italy was left with bombed-out cities and ruined farmland. Yet, within a few years, a new Italy emerged from the postwar destruction as the Italian Republic. Called "an economic miracle" by observers, the nation transformed itself from a poor and largely agricultural country into a major industrial power. Booming businesses manufactured and exported products to other parts of Europe, to Asia, and to North and South America.

As Italy built a new economy, it also struggled to find a new identity. Many people still picture quaint Renaissance villages and

old-fashioned farms when they think of Italy. Although Italians are proud of their past, they also seek recognition for their nation's modern contributions to the international economic and cultural community. These contributions have included sophisticated fashion and design, sleek automobiles, revolutionary films, and contemporary art and literature.

Italy has already overcome many divisions and obstacles as it has sought its place in the modern world, but it still has many challenges ahead. Throughout the last half of the twentieth century, unemployment, crime, an uneven distribution of wealth, and political scandal plagued the country. As Italy strides ahead in the twenty-first century, it will attempt to address these problems. At the same time, the nation is moving toward being part of a modern, unified Europe. In 2002, Italy became one of twelve European nations to adopt the euro. The euro is a new European currency shared by all of the participating countries. With steps like these, Italy continues on the road to stability, prosperity, and a promising future.

This model 550 Barchetta Pininfarina from **Ferrari** debuted in 2001. The Ferrari factory in Maranello, Italy, assembled all 448 of these limited edition vehicles.

THE LAND

The Italian Republic is situated in southern Europe on a long, narrow peninsula that juts into the Mediterranean Sea. The Alps, Europe's largest mountain range, form the country's northern boundary. Along this archlike border lie France and Monaco in the west, Switzerland and Austria in the north, and Slovenia in the east. Two independent states—Vatican City and the Republic of San Marino—lie within Italy's borders.

Four seas—each part of the greater Mediterranean—surround the Italian Peninsula. The Adriatic Sea lies to the east, while the Ionian Sea separates Italy from Greece in the southeast. The Tyrrhenian Sea is located off Italy's southwestern coast, and waves from the Ligurian Sea lap against the country's northwestern coast.

Italy covers a total of 116,320 square miles (301,269 square kilometers), including Sicily and Sardinia and other smaller islands. In area the country is slightly smaller than the state of New Mexico. From northwest to southeast, it is 708 miles (1,139 km), and the country measures 320 miles (515 km) across at its widest point in the north.

▶ Topography

Approximately three-quarters of Italy's terrain is mountainous, but the country's wide variety of geographical features ranges from smoldering volcanoes to serene lakes. Despite the diversity of the land, however, Italy has limited natural resources and relies on imports to fill many of its needs. Politically, Italy is divided into twenty administrative regions. The chief regions of the north are Piedmont, Lombardy, the Veneto, and Emilia-Romagna; of central Italy are Tuscany, Umbria, and Lazio; and of the south are Campania, Calabria, and Sicily. These areas follow traditional or historical boundaries but sometimes also match specific geographical features, such as mountain ranges or rivers.

The Alps dominate northern Italy's horizon as they sweep across central Europe. Many smaller ranges exist within the Alps, including the Maritime Alps, which divide Italy from France in the northwest. Mount Bianco in the Savoy Alps straddles the French-Italian border. It

Famous for their steep cliffs and dramatic hues, the Dolomites, an Alpine range near the Austrian border, were once part of an underwater reef. Marine fossils found among their spires and slopes date back to the Triassic Period more than 200 million years ago.

reaches an elevation of 15,771 feet (4,807 meters), the highest point in the Alps.

To the east, another series of Alpine ranges lies between Italy, Switzerland, and Austria. Northern Italy also features a line of Alpine lakes that were formed tens of thousands of years ago by melting glaciers (moving ice masses), and several glaciers still cover some of the area's high valleys. Travel within the Italian Alps is possible by way of a number of mountain passes, including the Brenner, the Great Saint Bernard, and the Little Saint Bernard.

Alpine foothills gradually descend to the flat and fertile Po Valley, Italy's largest plain, which spreads across the north central section of the country. With the exception of its Adriatic coastline, the Po Valley is entirely surrounded by mountains. Watered by the Po River, the valley has been settled and heavily farmed since ancient times and remains a densely populated area. The west central portion of the plain is Italy's industrial heartland but also supports many prosperous farms. The countryside of the northeastern valley is dotted with orchards and vineyards.

Just south of the Po Valley, the peaks of the Apennines run in a long north-south band all the way through central and into southern Italy. Generally lower and less steep than the Alps, the Apennines are thickly forested and host an abundance of wildlife. These mountains reach their highest point at Mount Corno.

Europe's southernmost **glacier** lies in Italy's Apennine Mountains.

On the western side of the peninsula, along the Tyrrhenian coast, plains provide rich farmland second in production only to the Po Valley. Farther south, these natural plains are supplemented by *maremme* (drained marshes), which farmers have made into fertile farmland.

A third plain sits on the Adriatic coast in southeastern Italy. Although extremely dry, the soil can be planted with crops such as olive trees, and farmers have terraced the land by cutting out plateaus (level areas) that butt against the cliffs of the Mediterranean coastline. In contrast, the steep hillsides at the southernmost tip of the peninsula support only small, relatively poor farms.

Sicily and Sardinia are the two largest islands in the Mediterranean. Separated from the mainland by the narrow Strait of Messina, the mountainous island of Sicily includes several rugged plateaus. Its highest point is Mount Etna, an active volcano near the eastern coast. Sardinia, in the Tyrrhenian Sea west of the Italian mainland, consists of the narrow Plain of Campidano, lined on either side by mountains. Sheepherding and other agricultural activities are important to this area.

ITALY'S FURNACES

Geologists estimate that Mount Etna has been active for more than 2.5 million years. Residents of ancient Sicily incorporated the fiery volcano into their myths, and people continue to admire and respect this unpredictable giant. Serious eruptions in the summer of 2001 threatened resorts and towns with hot ash and lava.

In A.D. 79, another Italian volcano, Mount Vesuvius, erupted and buried the city of Pompeii. Archaeologists have established that more than 3,360 people died.

Hot ash from Mount Vesuvius mummified this body in Pompeii. Mount Vesuvius last erupted in 1944. For links to more on Italy's volcanoes, visit vgsbooks.com.

This **NASA night view of the Po Valley** features Milan's cluster of yellow lights *(bottom center)*. Winding strings of yellow light represent mountain passes through the snow-covered Alps.

Other islands in the Tyrrhenian include the Lipari Islands, which sit north of Sicily. Capri and Ischia are situated near the Bay of Naples, and Elba lies off the coast of Tuscany.

▶ Rivers and Lakes

The Po River is Italy's longest waterway and passes through the nation's largest and most fertile agricultural area. The river flows eastward from the Alpine foothills through the lowlands of Lombardy and the Veneto.

As the Po approaches the Adriatic Sea, the river branches into a wide delta (a triangular piece of land formed by deposits of sediment at the mouth of the river). Many tributaries flow into the Po from the Alps in the north and from the Apennines in the south. In the spring, these smaller rivers, such as the Dora Baltea and the Taro, swell with rain and melted snow from the mountains. Rivers in the Alps and the Apennines have been harnessed for hydroelectric production for more than a century.

Italy's other major rivers include the Arno—the main waterway of Tuscany—and the Tiber, which drains the countryside of west central Italy around the nation's capital city of Rome. The Volturno is the largest and longest river in Campania. Many short rivers on the eastern side of the Apennines empty into the Adriatic Sea. These rivers often dry up during the warm summer months.

Thousands of years ago, Alpine glaciers in northern Italy formed a series of long, narrow lakes, including Lake Maggiore, Lake Como, and Lake Garda. In the central portion of the country, Lake Bolsena and Lake Bracciano fill the craters of extinct volcanoes north of Rome. Small mountain lakes dot the Apennines, and other lakes lie along the Adriatic coast. All of these spots attract tourists in the summer.

Climate

Italy's climate varies greatly from region to region. Temperatures and rainfall differ from north to south, from the high mountains to the low valleys, and from the coast to inland areas.

In the Po Valley, damp winters and warm summers are typical. Most rain falls in the spring and autumn. In the winter, the Alps and the high plateaus north of the Po Valley are blanketed by heavy snowfalls—as much as 30 feet (9 m) annually. More rain and snow fall in the northeast than in the northwest, where mild, dry winds blow in from the Mediterranean Sea. The city of Milan, on the plain of Lombardy, sees average temperatures of 39°F (4°C) in January and 73°F (23°C) in July.

Farther south the climate becomes warmer and drier, though at higher elevations temperatures generally are lower and precipitation is heavier than on the coastal plains. In Rome, which lies on the western plain not far from the Tyrrhenian Sea, temperatures average 45°F (7°C) in January and 78°F (26°C) in July. The Apennines shelter the Tyrrhenian coast from cold northerly winds, but this coast receives more rainfall than the Adriatic coast does.

Most of coastal Italy has a temperate Mediterranean climate. Rainfall is heaviest in the cool season, while the summers are almost rainless. Southern Italy and Sicily have dry, warm climates. Summers can be very hot, but winters are mild. Average rainfall in this region varies drastically, ranging from 20 to 40 inches (51 to 102 centimeters) or more, and is heavier near the coasts than it is in the mountainous interior. A hot wind, called a sirocco, blows northward into Italy from the deserts of northern Africa. In the spring, siroccos can even bring dust to southern portions of the Italian Peninsula.

Flora and Fauna

Italy has been settled for thousands of years. As a result, many of its woodlands have been cleared to make room for farms and cities. Yet natural forests still thrive in many of the nation's mountainous regions. The slopes of the Alps support beech, cypress, and oak trees. Shrubs, mosses, lichens, and many kinds of wildflowers grow above the tree line, where the climate is too extreme to support the growth of trees.

Some of Italy's rarest wildlife makes its home in **Abruzzi National Park**, located in the central **Apennine Mountains**. Since 1923 the park has fought to protect endangered plants and animals. Lucky visitors may glimpse the Apennine wolf, the Abruzzi chamois (a small antelope), or even the park's symbol, the Marsican brown bear.

As this ancient Roman mosaic from a villa in Sicily shows, **wild boars** have inhabited the Italian peninsula for at least two thousand years.

Centuries of farming and settlement have destroyed nearly all of the original forests in the lowlands of the Po Valley, but stands of poplar trees dot the countryside. In the Apennines, oak and chestnut forests are common. The dry highlands and coastal areas of the southeastern plain support hardy olive trees, as well as carob trees and Aleppo pines. Maquis, a type of scrub vegetation, grows in deforested regions of southern Italy, Sicily, and Sardinia.

The Alps are home to many of Italy's wild animals, including chamois, brown bears, foxes, roe deer, and ibexes. Otters and wildcats live in the Apennines, and a small number of wolves inhabit both central and southern Italy. Moufflon sheep and wild boars thrive in the rugged mountains of Sardinia.

At one time, Italian forests held millions of birds, but extensive hunting over the centuries has driven many species from the area. Grouse, ravens, and swallows are still common throughout the country. Hawks, falcons, and eagles can sometimes be spotted, and Sardinia is home to flocks of pink flamingos. Off the coasts, the Mediterranean suffers from pollution but still shelters sharks, octopi, tuna, swordfish, and several varieties of coral.

Cities

Italy is largely an urban nation. Although the country has a strong agricultural tradition, cities historically have been the most important political units on the Italian Peninsula. This trend continues in modern times, and approximately 90 percent of Italy's 57.8 million people reside in urban areas.

ROME Italy's capital and largest city, Rome (city population 2.7 million) lies along the banks of the Tiber River near the western coastal plain. The origins of Rome date back more than 2,700 years, when a collection of small, fortified farming villages covered several hills near the river. Eventually, Rome expanded, raised powerful armies, and conquered the Italian Peninsula.

During the fifth century A.D., the city came under the control of Roman Catholic popes. Over the following centuries, Rome became the center of the Catholic Church and of a domain known as the Papal States. In 1870, nearly a decade after Italy was unified, Rome was one of the last regions to be incorporated into the new state. Vatican City in central Rome has remained the independent domain of the Catholic Pope.

The modern city of Rome maintains hundreds of historical monuments, churches, and public buildings, as well as many museums showcasing a wealth of art and artifacts. The political and historical center of Italy, Rome is also an important hub of business, education, the arts, and entertainment. The Italian film and television industry, for example, is headquartered on the outskirts of the city. The University of Rome is Italy's largest institution of postsecondary education.

MILAN With a population of 1.3 million, Milan is the second largest city in Italy. Located on the northern plains, Milan is also the nation's business capital and an important European center of banking, service industries, and manufacturing. Milan prospered from trade with northern Europe during the time of the Roman Empire and grew in importance during the unification of Italy in the 1860s. About a century later, the city's many manufacturing firms drew immigrants from southern Italy. Modern Milan is the home of Italy's main stock exchange as well as la Scala, a world-famous opera house. Milan's Pirelli Tower, a modern glass skyscraper, is one of the tallest buildings in Italy.

Milan's gothic cathedral, (or *duomo* in Italian), was built to accommodate 40,000 worshipers. It also houses 3,400 statues.

GERMANY

SLOVAKIA

LIECHTENSTEIN

AUSTRIA

HUNGARY

SWITZERLAND

A L P S

Brenner Pass

Mount
Marmolada

DOLOMITES

Mount
Bianco

Great Saint
Bernard Pass

Dora

Little Saint
Bernard Pass

Baltea
River

Lake Como

SLOVENIA

Lake
Maggiore

Lake
Garda

CROATIA

Po River

Lake

Po River

Po

Valley

FRANCE

MARITIME ALPS

Taro River

San
Marino

BOSNIA
AND
HERZEGOVINA

MONACO

Arno River

A D R I A T I C   S E A

LIGURIAN
SEA

A P E N N I N E S

ELBA

Lake
Bolsena

CORSICA
[FRANCE]

Lake
Bracciano

Tiber River

Mount
Corno

VATICAN
CITY

Volturno R.

Mount Vesuvius

ISCHIA

SARDINIA

CAPRI

Plain of
Campidano

TYRRHENIAN
SEA

IONIAN
SEA

Italy

LIPARI
ISLANDS

Feet	Meters	
9843	3000	Mountains
6582	2000	Uplands
3281	1000	
1640	500	Lowlands

Elevation

Mount Etna

SICILY

Strait of
Messina

N

——— International border

▲ Mountain peak

)(Mountain pass

ALGERIA

0   100 Miles

0   100 KM

M E D I T E R R A N E A N   S E A

TUNISIA

NAPLES The manufacturing hub of Naples (population 1 million) lies on the north side of the Bay of Naples in southwestern Italy. The modern city suffers from overcrowding, crime, air pollution, and unemployment, but it was once a favorite summer resort for wealthy Roman families. Its elaborate cathedrals, ornate palaces, and imposing castles still draw tourists from around the world.

FLORENCE Rising along the fertile banks of the Arno River, Florence (population 377,000) is the birthplace of the Renaissance, a cultural movement that spanned the thirteenth through the sixteenth centuries. Artworks from this time period, such as Michelangelo's *David*, attract millions of viewers annually. Contemporary Florence is home also to many artists who carry on the city's tradition of fine handicrafts. Railroad, manufacturing, and communications industries also thrive in Florence.

VENICE Built in the center of a lagoon at the northern rim of the Adriatic Sea, Venice (population 291,500) was founded by refugees fleeing invasion and chaotic conditions on the mainland as early as the fifth century A.D. The Venetians constructed their unique city by sinking thousands of heavy wooden pilings into the surrounding lagoon and building on top of the pilings. Residents and visitors travel from place to place through a system of canals. Private boats, water taxis, and long, black rowboats known as gondolas serve as police vehicles, school buses, delivery vehicles, and nearly everything else. The many fine palaces, churches, and art galleries in Venice draw millions of visitors each year, making tourism by far the city's most important economic activity.

Scientists are concerned that Venice may sink up to 8 inches (20 cm) in the next fifty years. The city sank 5 inches (13 cm) in the last century.

HISTORY AND GOVERNMENT

Italy was first settled by hunters from northern and eastern Europe who crossed the Alps in search of game, and some artifacts suggest that humans may have inhabited the area as long ago as two hundred thousand years. The descendants of these people eventually spread down the length of the Italian Peninsula, stopping in fertile valleys to farm crops of grain and vegetables.

A group called the Etruscans began to establish twelve fortified city-states on the western plains of Italy in the 800s B.C. This territory came to be called Etruria (modern Tuscany). Skilled sculptors, potters, and metalworkers, the Etruscans traded goods with Greece, Egypt, and Phoenicia—a wealthy empire based in present-day Lebanon. As a result of all this trading and mining activity, great wealth accumulated in these Etruscan city-states, which formed a league ruled by kings and magistrates. Over time the Etruscans extended their holdings northward into the Po Valley and southward along the Tyrrhenian coast.

In the 700s B.C., Greeks seeking to escape overcrowded cities in their homeland settled in Sicily and southern Italy. This area, known to the Greeks as Magna Graecia (Greater Greece), was centered in Syracuse, a Sicilian city. The Greeks survived by trading consumer and agricultural products.

Etruria to Rome

One of the wealthiest areas under Etruscan control was Rome, a populous farming region that covered seven hills along the Tiber River. Until the end of the sixth century B.C., the Etruscan Tarquin dynasty (a family of rulers) controlled the region. In about 510 B.C., the Tarquin king was overthrown by the Senate, a body of Roman aristocrats who governed the city. The Senate founded a republic, in which two elected consuls served one-year terms as heads of state and as chief magistrates.

Outside of Rome, Etruscan rule remained intact for another seventy years, eventually weakening under the threat of foreign invasions.

The stone figures that recline on **Etruscan sarcophagi (coffins)** are famous for their expressive and delicately carved features.

Etruria gradually declined in power, and, by about 400 B.C., the armies of Rome had absorbed the area once held by the Etruscans and had added it to the republic's territory. The growing republic extended as far north as Tuscany and southward to Magna Graecia and Sicily. Backed by a large army, the Roman Senate soon ruled the entire Italian Peninsula.

As the city of Rome's power began to grow, power among its people remained unevenly divided. Roman society consisted of three main classes—patricians (aristocrats), plebians (common people), and slaves. The patricians ran the government, made laws, and imposed taxes—mostly on the plebians. Unsatisfied with their position, the plebians rebelled and gradually gained more power. They were eventually granted the right to help elect Rome's consuls and by 367 B.C. they were allowed to run for election themselves. The slave class, which lacked even basic rights under Roman law, grew along with Rome as more slaves were brought to the city from conquered lands.

In the third century B.C., Rome was threatened by armies from the North African city of Carthage (in present-day Tunisia). Troops crossed the Mediterranean to attack Sicily, an action that sparked a series of wars against Rome that lasted for more than one hundred years.

The clashes between Carthage and Rome, collectively known as the Punic Wars, featured many invasions and counterinvasions. In 218 B.C., the Carthaginian general Hannibal entered Italy from the north and attacked Roman cities. Roman armies fought back and defeated Hannibal, a victory that allowed the republic to extend its authority to the Mediterranean islands of Sicily, Sardinia, and Corsica, as well as to the northern coast of Africa—including Carthage. The end of the Punic Wars left Rome supreme in the Mediterranean. In addition to its previous holdings, Roman military leaders added Greece and Egypt to the republic.

Rome's expanding colonial power brought great wealth to the patricians. But heavy taxation, land shortages, and the massive enlistment of the lower classes in the Roman army sparked revolts among plebians and slaves. The brothers Tiberius and Gaius Gracchus, two liberal-minded leaders, led a reform movement meant to extend greater freedoms and rights to disadvantaged members of Roman society. After reform attempts were squelched—and the brothers were assassinated—civil war erupted between Roman landowners and laborers.

The civil wars led to deep divisions within the Roman Senate. Crassus and Pompey, senators who had helped to put down the revolts, formed a triumvirate (a ruling association of three) with Julius Caesar, a successful Roman general. After the death of Crassus, Caesar defeated Pompey in battle and named himself the sole ruler of Rome. In 51 B.C., Caesar conquered Gaul (present-day France), adding European lands west of the Rhine River to the Roman Republic.

Fearing Caesar's dictatorship, several of his former allies murdered him in 44 B.C. Thirteen years later, Caesar's nephew Octavian defeated rivals at the naval Battle of Actium, off the coast of Greece. The Senate then proclaimed Octavian ruler of the Roman Empire.

Roman Rise and Fall

Under the title Augustus, Octavian ordered the building of new roads and public-works projects throughout the empire, which included most of Europe and the Middle East and parts of North Africa. His administration also established a uniform system of law for use throughout the vast domain. Roman culture and Latin (the language of the Romans) spread to the empire's far corners.

Augustus's successors reigned during the Pax Romana, a two-hundred-year period when the realm enjoyed stability and peace. Laborers raised great walls on the northern frontiers to protect Roman conquests. Fortifications were built along the Rhine and Danube Rivers in central Europe for additional security.

Meanwhile, the new religion of Christianity was rapidly gaining popularity among Roman citizens, even though it was not legal. Victims of persecution under the early emperors, Christians had become the dominant religious group within the

To protect the empire's territory in England, the Roman emperor Hadrian ordered the construction of a great stone wall in about A.D. 122. Originally Hadrian's Wall stretched more than 70 miles (113 km) and was about 16 feet (5 m) high. Large parts of the wall and nearby ruins can still be seen in northern England.

empire by the fourth century. A bishop, or local church leader, held authority in many Roman cities, including Rome itself. In A.D. 313, during the reign of Emperor Constantine, the Edict of Milan legalized Christianity.

In 330 Constantine founded a second capital, Constantinople (present-day Istanbul, Turkey), to serve as an administrative hub for the empire's eastern regions. While the Italian Peninsula remained the center of the Western Empire, Constantinople became the seat of the Eastern Empire, later known as the Byzantine Empire. The city also became a new center of the Christian faith. Christian leaders in Rome and Constantinople eventually developed different rituals and doctrines and became rivals for the loyalty of Christian worshipers throughout the empire.

Emperor Constantine

Geographic divisions were not the only challenge to the empire's stability. Waves of Goths and other Germanic peoples from northern Europe had begun to invade western and southern Europe. Their arrival, and their success in beating Rome's armies, caused the frontiers of the Western Roman Empire to shrink. In 410 an army of Visigoths overran Rome, looting the treasury and burning the capital's monuments. Roman rule soon ended in Gaul, Spain, and North Africa. The Gothic leader Odoacer overthrew the last Roman emperor in 476 and seized the leadership of the declining realm. By the end of the fifth century, the Western Empire had collapsed.

Byzantine and Lombard Rule

Despite the fall of Roman rule, Roman-style administration and culture survived in Italy. Many cities succeeded in absorbing the invading groups, some of whom eventually converted to Christianity and began to follow Roman laws and customs.

At the same time, rulers of the Byzantine Empire sought to assert their control over the Italian Peninsula and in the mid-sixth century they successfully campaigned against the Goths. Ravenna, a city on the Adriatic coast, became the seat of Byzantine power in Italy, and the emperor Justinian officially made Italy a Byzantine province in 554.

Within about a decade, the Lombards, another Germanic group, had swept westward into the Po Valley from what would

This sixth century A.D. mosaic of Byzantine **emperor Justinian** *(center)* graces a wall in Ravenna's Saint Vitale Church.

become Hungary. They founded a new capital in the north at Pavia and gradually settled across much of Italy. Lombard kings and dukes captured Ravenna with their armies, ending Byzantine rule in Italy. They then built a string of semi-independent states.

Rivalry developed between the Lombard kings and the Pope, the leader of the Roman Catholic Church. Catholic popes had replaced the emperors as the rulers of Rome and its surrounding area and were using this region as a base for spreading the Church's authority to the rest of Italy. But, without military force, the popes were unable to control the Lombard rulers.

In the 750s, as Lombard power grew, the popes turned to foreign rulers to defend Rome. Pope Stephen II asked for help from the Franks, whose kingdom included much of western Europe. Pepin III, the Frankish king, defeated the Lombards and turned Ravenna over to the Pope. Pepin's donation of lands became the basis for the Papal States. Although the boundaries of the Papal States would change often, they remained under the control of the Roman Catholic Church into the nineteenth century. In 774, during the reign of Pepin's son Charlemagne, the Frankish armies overthrew the Lombard king Desiderius and added the northern region of Lombardy to Charlemagne's empire. In gratitude Pope Leo III crowned Charlemagne emperor of the Romans in 800. By this time,

Even before being crowned by the Pope, **Charlemagne** was one of Europe's most important and enlightened leaders. As ruler of a huge empire, he sought to bring reform and order to his territories, to boost commerce and agriculture, to inspire artistic and cultural creativity, and to improve and promote education.

Charlemagne's kingdom extended from northeastern Spain and central Italy northward to Denmark.

After Charlemagne died in 814, rivalries among his successors caused turmoil. In 843 the Treaty of Verdun divided the Carolingian realm (Charlemagne's kingdom) among three descendants. For more than a century, the Carolingians fought one another for control of the kingdom.

Meanwhile, in the south, wealthy dukes and landowners continued to run their lands independently. The region was weakly defended, however, and in the ninth century Sicily, Sardinia, and the port of Bari on the southern Adriatic coast fell to Arab invaders from North Africa.

Rivalries and the Renaissance

Rivalry among princes and dukes for control of northern Italy brought foreign intervention again in the tenth century. Fearing a loss of control over papal territories, Pope John XII crowned the German king Otto I as Holy Roman Emperor and gave him charge of the Holy Roman Empire. In theory this coronation made Otto the leader of Europe's Christian states, although most people in the empire also remained loyal to local princes. Through his alliance with the Pope, Otto held authority over both church and state in most of Italy.

Later popes competed with the monarchs of Germany for control of Italian affairs. Although the German princes elected the German king, the Pope crowned his choice as the Holy Roman Emperor. In turn the emperor appointed new popes, bishops, and other important Church officials.

But many Catholics felt that the Church should name its own leaders

Holy Roman Emperor Otto I

without the help of German royalty. A series of power struggles resulted between the monarchy and the papacy. A compromise between the Holy Roman Emperor and Church officials came about in 1122. The Concordat of Worms took the appointment of Church officials out of the control of the emperors, who were still recognized as the legitimate civilian rulers of Italy.

The rivalry between the popes and the emperors left Italian cities free to assert their independence from both authorities. Through trading and banking, Milan, Florence, Venice, Genoa, Pisa, and others developed into wealthy city-states. An emerging middle class made up of merchants and artisans formed powerful political factions within these northern city-states, competing with farmers and aristocrats for control of local government. With their growing wealth and military power, the city-states were able to absorb surrounding estates and farmland and become entirely self-sufficient.

Farther south, various European powers vied for control of southern Italy and Sicily from the eleventh to the thirteenth centuries. By the late 1200s, Spain held Sicily, while the French controlled Naples.

Despite political turmoil and economic setbacks in the 1300s, by the early 1400s manufacturing and trade had made several city-states in Italy among the wealthiest communities in Europe. To glorify their achievements, the leaders of Florence, Rome, Venice, and other cities hired skilled artists to decorate homes, churches, and public buildings. Universities flourished in Padua and Bologna, where scholars translated the works of ancient Greek and Roman playwrights, philosophers, and historians. Italy's artists and writers turned to the classical past as inspiration for their works, resulting in a rebirth, or Renaissance, of art and learning that gradually spread to the rest of Europe.

The Doge's Palace was home to the ruler of Venice. Much of its ornate interior detail work *(left)* was completed during the Renaissance.

THE DARK SIDE OF PROSPERITY

In 1347 rats on trading ships from the Black Sea spread the bubonic plague, or the black death, to Italy. Within five years, it had killed twenty-five million people in Europe. The author Giovanni Boccaccio described the effects of the disease on his hometown of Florence:

Oh, how many great palaces, beautiful homes, and noble dwellings, once filled with families, gentle-men, and ladies, were now emp-tied, down to the last ser-vant! . . . How many valiant men, beautiful women, and charming young men . . . dined in the morning with their relatives, companions, and friends and then in the evening took supper with their ancestors in the other world!

—from *The Decameron* (translated by Mark Musa and Peter E. Bondanella)

At the same time, the governments of many city-states were under the control of local dictators, called *signori*. A few signori were appointed by the community, while some stepped in to reestablish order after civil strife. Many signori founded family dynasties that remained in control for centuries.

Other city-states were guided by small groups of wealthy merchants. The Medici family, which ran an international banking business, was prominent in Florence. Venice, on the other hand, controlled a network of trading ports in the Adriatic and Mediterranean. The city's council, senate, and head of state (known as a doge) ran civic affairs. This system protected Venice's interests and brought the port city many centuries of political stability.

◉ Foreign Invasions

In the mid-fifteenth century, the drive to expand and control ever larger territories brought the city-states into conflict with one another and with outside powers such as France, Spain, and Germany. The Italian city-states signed the Peace of Lodi in 1454 to settle their differences, but the peace was short-lived. In 1494 an army of thirty thousand French soldiers sent by King Charles VIII invaded Milan and continued down the peninsula to Naples.

French and Spanish armies continued to fight over territory in southern Italy for years. In 1519 King Charles of Spain, who was a member of the Habsburg family, became the Holy Roman Emperor. As a result, from the start of Charles's reign, the Habsburg Empire ruled Italy. By 1560 his heirs officially controlled most of the Italian Peninsula.

Spanish rule was harsh. Italian cities struggled under the burden of growing taxes and heavy-handed administrators, especially in the south, where peasant revolts broke out during the 1600s. Banking and manufacturing business declined, and poor harvests brought outbreaks of famine and disease.

During the 1700s, the powerful states of Europe began to use Italy as a battlefield and its states as bargaining chips to strike a balance of power among themselves. Austria gradually came to influence northern Italy, while Spain continued to hold the south. The Catholic Church remained in control of Rome and the Papal States.

In the early 1790s, following a popular rebellion in France that had ended the French monarchy, Italy's republicans (people who favored representative government without a king) also rebelled. Italy's foreigners, powerful princes, and merchant families harshly put down the revolts. By the spring of 1796, however, republican armies under the French leader Napoleon Bonaparte had swept across northern Italy.

Napoleon Bonaparte

The new French government reorganized Italy. In place of many small city-states, Napoleon created the Kingdom of Italy, naming himself as king. He introduced a central administration and a uniform set of laws known as the Napoleonic Code. The kingdom seized Church properties and large estates, built new roads, and established a centralized educational system.

But Europe's powerful monarchies were determined not to allow Napoleon to succeed. Britain, Austria, Prussia (part of Germany), Russia, and Spain allied their armies and defeated Napoleon in 1815. The victors then met to divide Italy. Lombardy and Venetia went to Austria. Spain got Sicily and Naples in the south. The dukes of Savoy gained Genoa and Piedmont (regions near present-day France), which, together with Sardinia, became the Kingdom of Sardinia, later known as Sardinia-Piedmont.

◉ Risorgimento and Unification

In spite of Napoleon's defeat, many republican leaders were still determined to establish a unified, independent Italian state. They formed secret nationalist societies that conspired against the foreign-led administrations of Italy. This Risorgimento (reawakening) movement gained followers among people frustrated by the failure of popular revolts in southern Italy and in Savoy and Genoa.

A wave of rebellions swept across Europe in 1848 as workers, students, and revolutionaries stormed the streets of European capitals to demand representative governments. The unrest inspired workers in Venice and Milan to act, but Austrian armies forcefully put down the riots.

Although temporarily defeated, the Italian nationalists did not give up. They turned to the independent monarchy of Sardinia-Piedmont, whose king, Victor Emmanuel II, supported Italian unification. An opponent of Austria, he saw unification as a way to give Italy its own voice, to oust Austria, and to gain some of Austria's holdings on the Italian Peninsula.

In the 1850s, Camillo Benso di Cavour, the prime minister of Sardinia-Piedmont, secretly negotiated with France, Austria's rival. In return for the regions of Savoy and Nice, the French gave military support to Sardinia-Piedmont. In 1859 forces from Sardinia-Piedmont and France defeated the Austrian army.

By the Treaty of Villafranca signed by France and Austria, Austria surrendered Lombardy to France, which then ceded the region to Sardinia-Piedmont. But, although France had supported actions to weaken Austria, it did not approve of Italian unification. To Cavour's disappointment, important regions such as Tuscany and Emilia remained under the control of rulers allied with Austria. To express his dissatisfaction with this agreement, Cavour resigned.

Giuseppe Garibaldi *(center, seated)* directs his red-shirted soldiers in battle.

Motivated to continue fighting for a republic, Italian rebels planned another revolt. Giuseppe Garibaldi organized a military band known as the Thousand. When rebellion broke out in Sicily, the Thousand sailed to the island and quickly overthrew its Spanish administration. Garibaldi then led the group on a march to Naples, forcing the Spaniards to abandon the city.

Garibaldi's campaign sparked nationalist rebellions throughout Italy. Cavour returned to office in Sardinia-Piedmont and again negotiated with France. French officials agreed to support a new constitutional monarchy in Italy if the Pope and Rome remained self-governing.

In October 1860, Victor Emmanuel II entered Naples, where Garibaldi presented him with the lands of Sicily and southern Italy and proclaimed him king. By a popular vote, provinces in central and southern Italy joined the kingdom. The new Italian parliament announced the kingdom's founding on March 17, 1861. Rome continued to be self-ruling but had the protection of the French military, Venetia stayed under Austrian control, and San Marino remained an independent republic. The rest of the Italian Peninsula, along with Sardinia-Piedmont and Sicily, formed the Kingdom of Italy.

Italy, suddenly a unified nation, began playing an important role in Europe's complex power struggles. When Austria faced off against Prussia in 1866, Italy allied with Prussia. The Prussian victory allowed the Italian kingdom to annex Venetia. Four years later, during the Franco-Prussian War (1870–1871), France withdrew its military from Rome. Italian troops quickly seized the city, which was chosen to be the capital of Italy.

◉ Decades of Turmoil

Although Italy experienced changes in its governmental structure during the 1800s, the country remained largely agricultural and could not compete with the rapidly industrializing nations of western Europe. In the south, where the old system of landownership had survived until the early nineteenth century, poverty-stricken peasants still farmed meager holdings. Unrest stirred in southern Italy and Sicily, where riots and crime became commonplace.

Poor social and economic conditions in the late 1800s and early 1900s sent millions of Italian emigrants, most of them from the south, in search of better lives. It is estimated that nearly five million Italians arrived in the United States between 1875 and 1913.

Italy also suffered from a lack of strong political leadership. The kingdom's constitution gave only a small percentage of men from the upper classes the right to vote. This group dominated the legislature without addressing the country's widespread social problems. In addition, Italy's politicians formed dozens of parties that constantly combined and recombined into different coalitions. With a wide variety of political beliefs, these groups could not agree on a common policy to improve the economy or the standard of living among Italy's workers and farmers.

New political factions, such as the Socialist Party, established themselves with the support of farmers and urban laborers. Dissatisfied with the political system, these new organizations led strikes (work stoppages). Rioting among the urban poor shook Rome and cities around the nation several times in the 1890s. Similar social unrest occurred in Sicily.

In 1900 Giovanni Giolitti, a liberal-minded reformist, became Italy's prime minister. Under Giolitti the Italian parliament legalized strikes, passed child labor laws, and limited the length of the work week. In 1912 the right to vote was extended to all adult males. (Women won this right in 1945.)

During Giolitti's term as prime minister, northern Italy experienced rapid growth in manufacturing and industry. At the same time, Italy sought to expand its power and territory by establishing colonies abroad. The nation had tried several times to take over Ethiopia, and by 1912 Italy had succeeded in taking over Eritrea (once part of Ethiopia) and Somaliland (present-day Somalia) in eastern Africa. Italy had also gained a tenuous hold on Libya in northern Africa.

As Italy's prime minister, **Giovanni Giolitti** oversaw reforms favorable to workers.

The quest for colonies, land, and economic advantage sparked strong rivalries among the states of Europe during the late nineteenth and early twentieth centuries. By 1914 European powers had formed two major military alliances. The Triple Entente included France, Britain, and Russia. In opposition to the Entente, Italy joined the Triple Alliance with Germany and Austria. By this agreement, the three states pledged to defend one another in case of attack.

In 1914 the assassination of the heir to the Austrian throne sparked World War I. In retaliation Austria attacked Serbia, a southeastern European nation that the Austrians believed was responsible for the murder. The war soon engulfed the two military alliances. German armies began fighting France and Russia. Italy chose to remain neutral, claiming that the Austrian attack violated certain terms of the Triple Alliance and was not an excuse for Italy's entry into the war. By the secret Treaty of London, signed in 1915, the Triple Entente promised Italy territorial gains if Italy would enter the war on the Entente's side.

The Italian government declared war on Austria in May 1915. Italian forces were unprepared for a major war and suffered defeat at the Battle of Caporetto in October 1917. But the tide of war had already turned against Austria and Germany. In November 1918, the Triple Alliance surrendered. The postwar Treaty of Versailles awarded Trieste and Trentino to Italy. But the treaty gave other regions that had been promised to Italy to the new state of Yugoslavia on the Balkan Peninsula.

Mussolini, Fascism, and World War II

World War I had claimed hundreds of thousands of Italian lives. War debt burdened the Italian economy, while unemployment rose in the cities. In 1919 Benito Mussolini, a war veteran and former newspaper editor, founded the political group Fasci di Combattimento (Combat Groups). In his speeches and writings, Mussolini expressed anger toward the Italian government, which many Italians considered ineffective in foreign policy and in economic and social programs. Many workers agreed and joined Mussolini's fascist organization, a group that supported a rigid, conservative political system.

The new Fascist Party leader also found growing support among the middle class and farmers. In 1922 Mussolini prepared to march on Rome. Fearing violence in the capital, King Victor Emmanuel III invited him to form a new government and to select a cabinet of ministers. Mussolini then proclaimed himself dictator of Italy under the title of Il Duce (The Leader). The Fascists quickly reorganized the Italian state and took control of the economy. Public-works projects brought full employment to workers, while newspapers were censored, and opponents of the regime were imprisoned.

By the 1930s, a fascist party under Adolf Hitler also had control of Germany. Mussolini sought an alliance with Germany as a means of expanding his empire. Italy invaded Ethiopia in 1935 and with Germany formed the Axis alliance the following year. The oppressive actions of Mussolini's government, however, made it increasingly unpopular among Italians. Strict press censorship, political repression, low standards of living in much of the country, and the persecution of Jews sparked increasing resistance to Italy's Fascist regime.

Hitler's efforts to annex (take over) territory led to the outbreak of World War II in 1939. Italy did not join the conflict right away but in 1940 declared war on France and Britain—Germany's enemies and part of the anti-Axis Allies. The Italian army quickly suffered a series of military setbacks that rendered it nearly powerless during the course of the war.

In July 1943, the Allies invaded Sicily and quickly overran the island. Italians opposed to Mussolini's regime fought on the Allied side, pushing northward toward Rome. The Fascist Grand Council (a political body in Mussolini's government) voted Mussolini out of office, and Italy formally joined the Allies and declared war on Germany.

Benito Mussolini *(center front)* leads his military staff.

After years of wartime hardship and military defeat, **Italian soldiers** in Sicily are glad to surrender to Allied forces near the end of World War II.

Determined to control the Italian Peninsula, German armies in Italy reinforced their lines and put up a stiff resistance, establishing Mussolini as the head of a puppet government in the north. In heavy fighting, the Allied armies slowly pushed the German lines northward. In April 1945, Mussolini attempted to flee the country but was caught and executed. Hitler committed suicide in the same month, and in May Germany surrendered.

Postwar Revival

In 1946 a national vote ended the Italian monarchy and founded the Italian Republic. But political turmoil continued. Debates and conflicts among Italy's many political parties frequently led to changes in government and to new elections.

By the late 1940s, the Italian political system had come to be dominated by the Christian Democratic Party, which included various coalitions. Socialists usually found themselves in a minority coalition. The Italian Communist Party benefited from a strong alliance with the Communist-run Soviet Union and often won a greater percentage of votes than the Socialist Party did. Yet Communist Party members were never invited into any governing coalition.

Fearing the growing power of the Italian Communists, the strongly anticommunist United States extended massive amounts of financial aid to Italy to strengthen its majority government. This aid allowed Italy to rebuild its cities, industries, and transportation systems, all of which had been severely damaged in the war. The Italian government also set up a fund to develop southern Italy, which lagged behind the rest of the country in its standard of living and in economic growth.

Italian prime minister Alcide De Gasperi *(right)* confers with British prime minister Sir Winston Churchill *(left)* in London in 1953.

Italy's links to the United States went beyond economic aid. In 1949, under Prime Minister Alcide De Gasperi, Italy joined the North Atlantic Treaty Organization (NATO), a military alliance of western European and North American nations. In 1957 Italy also became a member of the European Economic Community (a forerunner of the European Union), which lowered trade barriers among European member nations.

Cheap labor and rising exports brought a boom in Italian manufacturing industries in the late 1950s and early 1960s. Busy factories in Lombardy and Piedmont produced steel for new building construction, appliances, and automobiles. Wages rose rapidly for workers, and a large market helped farmers sell more of their produce.

But, in the mid-1960s, the Italian economy slowed. Heavy social spending by the government caused large budget shortfalls. As wages rose, prices for goods went up, and the standard of living began to stagnate. Communist and Socialist leaders who supported workers' rights were pushing for change and organizing large-scale, antigovernment strikes in Italian factories. In national elections, these parties won high percentages of the popular vote.

In 1974 the country suffered a severe blow when the oil-producing nations of the Middle East prohibited oil exports, an action that caused fuel shortages and inflation (rising prices) throughout Europe. Italy also experienced a wave of terrorism at the hands of a number of radical political groups throughout the 1970s. The Red Brigades, for example, carried out bombings and kidnapped business leaders and politicians. The social and economic chaos drew even more voters toward the Socialist Party.

Scandal and Reform

In 1983 Italy's first postwar Socialist government came to power under the leadership of Bettino Craxi, whose administration lasted until 1987. Throughout the 1980s, Italy's economy continued to grow despite inflation. By the early 1990s, however, many Italians were calling for fundamental reform of the political parties. The system of coalition governments seemed unable to cope with economic problems. In addition, a bribery scandal exposed corruption among many high-ranking politicians, business leaders, and judges. Despite hundreds of arrests and trials, many people believed that corruption remained commonplace among Italian leaders.

As the scandal widened, several new groups rose to challenge the traditional political system. These included the Lega Nord (Northern

These **Lega Nord** (Northern League) supporters carry flags at a political rally in the mid-1990s.

League), composed of regional leaders in northern Italy who sought independence from the central government, and Forza Italia (Go, Italy), a nationalist party led by business tycoon Silvio Berlusconi. In April 1994, a victory by Forza Italia allowed Berlusconi to form a new government.

Although the new prime minister announced measures to lessen the budget deficit, to reform the government, and to fight organized crime, he resigned in December when the governing coalition fell apart. Interim administrations and new elections led to a succession of short-lived and largely ineffective governments. General elections in 2001 brought Silvio Berlusconi back to power, with promises to cut taxes, restrict immigration, and boost law enforcement. Like all of Italy's leaders, Berlusconi must try to balance the interests and demands of the nation's people and the government's many parties. He must also secure the public's trust in the wake of lengthy investigations into his financial conduct and business dealings during the 1990s. Berlusconi faces allegations of conflicts of interest between his duties as prime minister and his many business enterprises.

In the meantime, Italy prepared for the adoption of the euro, a new European currency. Differences of opinion over this step toward a unified Europe caused turmoil in Berlusconi's cabinet, leading to the resignation of his foreign minister. When the euro officially entered circulation on January 1, 2002, Italians experienced long lines and difficult transactions as businesses and consumers made the switch. However, by April 2002, economy experts predicted dropping inflation levels and smoother transactions with the new currency.

Government

The constitution of the Italian Republic was passed in 1947 and went into effect January 1, 1948. The document established a 630-member Chamber of Deputies and a 315-member Senate. Together these bodies form Parliament. Adults eighteen years of age and older elect the deputies, while voters must be twenty-five years old to elect senators. Representatives of both houses serve five-year terms, but the number of seats held by each party is determined by the number of votes the party receives in national elections.

Go to vgsbooks.com for links to websites where you can find out more about the Roman Empire, the Italian Renaissance, Italy's government, and up-to-date news in Italy from various news organizations.

Italy's **Chamber of Deputies** meets in this ornate hall, designed and built in the early 1900s.

A two-thirds majority vote of the legislature chooses the president, who serves a term of seven years. The president acts as head of state and commander of the armed forces. As part of the legislative process, the president has the power to promulgate (declare) laws and to veto proposed legislation. The president can also call for special sessions of Parliament and for elections. However, many presidential actions must have the support of Parliament or the prime minister.

The Italian president appoints numerous positions within the government. For example, the president appoints the prime minister from the Chamber of Deputies. The prime minister, in turn, selects the members of the cabinet, who must be approved by Parliament. The prime minister's other duties include working with Parliament to decide on government policies and actions.

The cabinet and prime minister have no fixed terms of office, but Parliament can pass a vote of no confidence in the government and force the prime minister to resign. The president may also dissolve the government at any time. In either case, new elections are held.

Italy is divided into twenty regions, each of which includes provinces and municipalities. Elected councils and committees govern the provinces. The regional councils have broad authority to pass laws affecting planning, taxation, and other matters, but these laws may be revoked by the national government or the constitutional court.

The constitutional court includes fifteen appointed judges, each of whom serves a term of nine years. This court rules on laws passed by Parliament and by regional and local governments. Appeals courts hear civil and criminal cases from lower courts. Italy also has a system of tax courts and administrative courts.

THE PEOPLE

Italy has a population of 57.8 million people, but settlements are distributed unevenly across the country. The plains of Lombardy, Piedmont, and Lazio, for example, are densely populated, while the slopes of the Alps in the north, the Apennines, and southern Italy have fewer people. The country's overall population density is 497 people per square mile (192 per sq. km), compared to 278 per square mile (107 per sq. km) in the neighboring country of France and 77 per square mile (30 per sq. km) in the United States.

To find out more about the various customs of people in the different regions of Italy—including Veneto, Tuscany, Sicily, and more—to learn some basic Italian words, and to get Italy's most up-to-date population figures, visit vgsbooks.com.

web enhanced @ www.vgsbooks.com

Over the years, many villagers and farmers have moved into urban centers in search of employment. As a result, the rural areas of the country, especially in the southern regions of Calabria and Basilicata, have experienced a sharp decline in population. With about 90 percent of its people living in cities, Italy is one of the most heavily urbanized nations in the world.

Ethnic Groups

During its long history, Italy has been settled by many different peoples. As a result, the ethnic heritage of Italian citizens is widely varied. Minorities in Italy include the German-speaking residents of Alpine villages in the Trentino-Alto Adige region. There is also a Slovene population (originally from Slovenia) concentrated in the northeastern part of the country. Both of these groups have faced challenges and persecution in Italy, particularly during the Fascist regime and during World War II. In the last half of the twentieth century, the government granted some special rights to these ethnic minorities, such as the right to use their own languages in school. However, legislation varies from region to region. Slovenes in particular are dissatisfied with their status and have organized a number of groups to seek greater rights and freedoms. Another minority group is the Roma, often referred to as Gypsies. With origins in India about one thousand years ago, the Italian Roma have their own language and customs. They belong to a once-nomadic group that is spread throughout Europe and around the world. Victims of harsh discrimination and even violence in Italy, most Roma live in camps outside of major cities and remain largely isolated from mainstream society.

About 2 percent of the Italian population is foreign born. Beginning in the 1960s, various ethnic groups began immigrating to Italy to look for work in the country's expanding economy, and the country is home to more than one million of these legal immigrants. At the beginning of the twenty-first century, Italy continues to be a major European des-

This **Roma family** lives in Sardinia. Although many Roma have settled in towns and cities, their heritage as travelers is still important to their culture.

tination for people seeking better lives and working conditions than they have found in their homelands. Foreign laborers from North Africa, Asia, and the Middle East have settled in Rome, Milan, Turin, and Genoa. Instability and war in Albania and the former republics of Yugoslavia have brought a large population of refugees, especially to southern Italy. Each year boats and ships, some bearing hundreds of illegal immigrants and refugees from countries including India, Sri Lanka, Pakistan, China, and nations in eastern Europe, attempt to land on Italy's long, often under-patrolled coastline.

Language

Italian, like French and Spanish, is a Romance language with roots in ancient Latin. The language of the Roman Empire, Latin survived the empire's fall and became an international tongue of science, philosophy, and religion during the Middle Ages (A.D. 500–A.D. 1500). At the same time, the many separate regions of Italy developed their own local dialects, and the peninsula had no national spoken language until the late nineteenth century.

LA BELLA LINGUA (THE BEAUTIFUL LANGUAGE)

Although many dialects exist in Italy, most Italians can understand a standard, written form of the Italian language. Here are a few common Italian words and phrases translated into English:

ITALIAN	ENGLISH
gli amici	friends
arrivederci	good-bye (literally, "until we see each other again")
buon giorno	good day
il calcio	soccer
ciao	hello/good-bye (casual)
il gelato	ice cream
grazie	thank you
mi scusi	excuse me
prego	you're welcome

To learn more Italian or to read an Italian newspaper, visit vgsbooks.com for links.

Modern Italian developed in the thirteenth and fourteenth centuries from the dialect spoken in Florence. Centuries later the popularity of the language was boosted during the unification movement, when having a common language became a necessity. After World War II, the Roman dialect also spread through television and film.

Local dialects still survive in many areas of Italy, including Sicily, Naples, and Venice. People who speak one Italian dialect do not necessarily understand those who speak another. In addition, foreign languages are used in several border areas. In 1992 the Italian government recognized the official use of Sardinian and Friulian (a northeastern Italian language) in their respective areas. German is common near

An Italian family poses on the church steps for a **wedding photo.** Close-knit Italian families may include distant relatives as well as immediate family, so an Italian wedding can draw many people.

Austria, and French is heard in Piedmont and in the Valle d'Aosta. Speakers of Slovenian and Croatian live near the city of Trieste. Many Albanian and Greek immigrants in southern Italy also communicate in their native tongues.

Social Structure and Customs

Outside influences, a nearly constant influx of new people, and geographical isolation have made many Italians feel their greatest loyalty to their regions, their towns, or their families. Customs, values, language, and even local foods are all based on a wide range of factors that may differ widely from region to region.

One characteristic common to most Italians is a great love of and loyalty to family. In some areas, this value may mean that several generations of immediate family live together under one roof, while in others "family" refers even to distant relatives and possibly to close neighbors or friends as well. Italy's divorce rate is among the lowest in the world, and women are the traditional caregivers and homemakers in Italian households. A particularly strong bond between Italian mothers and their sons is nearly legendary.

Outside of the home, the role of Italian women is a controversial issue. The Italian feminist movement first began in the mid-1800s and had a strong revival in the 1960s and 1970s. The movement eventually helped women to achieve rights such as access to universities and the right to run for public office. Despite these advances, modern Italian women still face discrimination and challenges, including limited access to the workplace and lower pay than male counterparts. Violence toward women is also an ongoing problem, and lenient rulings in the late 1990s and early 2000s on rape and sexual harassment have stirred many Italian women to protest and to call for change.

Italian women of the twenty-first century struggle against discrimination in the workplace.

Pioneering Italian educator **Maria Montessori,** born in Chiaravalle, enjoyed working with children all her life.

Education

Italian education has a long history. A medical school was founded at Salerno around the tenth century A.D. The University of Bologna, established in about 1088, is the oldest European university still in operation. Throughout the Middle Ages and the Renaissance, more schools opened in Pisa, Florence, Rome, and other cities.

In the 1800s, the nation continued to make strides. Minister of Education Michele Coppino introduced a law in 1877 making elementary schooling compulsory. Maria Montessori raised new ideas about teaching in the 1900s. However, Italian education suffered under the Fascist regime, when classes neglected some subjects to focus on studying Fascist ideals.

After World War II, the Italian school system found itself unprepared for the task of educating the nation's growing population. A lack of facilities and teachers, as well as a disorganized educational network, contributed to the problems. Despite Coppino's law, many elementary-aged children did not attend school at all, and others who wanted to enroll were too poor to afford basic school supplies.

During the 1960s, the national government budgeted money to improve

LESSONS IN LEARNING

Maria Montessori (1870–1952) was a teacher and physician who proposed a new approach to education in the early 1900s. Through her successful work with young children in Rome's slums, she developed a system that emphasized allowing students to develop at their own pace. Montessori also encouraged hands-on learning. Her methods are used in many modern schools in Italy and around the world.

educational facilities and to hire many new teachers. School attendance rose, and illiteracy fell rapidly among school-aged children. By the end of the twentieth century, 98 percent of adult Italians could read and write.

Education is compulsory for children between the ages of six and fourteen. Students attend primary school from ages six to eleven and then go on to three years of lower secondary school. They then must pass a comprehensive examination to move to higher secondary schools, which are devoted to the studies of science, vocational skills, the arts, and the humanities.

After five years of higher secondary school, students take another test, called the *maturità*, that allows admission to any Italian university. The oldest of Italy's many universities is the University of Bologna, which dates to the eleventh century.

Health

Before World War II, Italy suffered a shortage of hospitals and trained physicians. Public health improved dramatically with the economic boom of the 1950s and the 1960s. Modern health services extend low-cost medical care, examinations, and medicines to all Italian citizens. In 2001 the rate of infant mortality (the number of babies who die within a year of their birth) was 5.2 per 1,000 live births, a figure below the southern European average of 7. Average life expectancy among Italians is 79 years, higher than the southern European average of 77 years.

The social welfare system in Italy provides disability payments, unemployment benefits, and retirement pensions to Italian workers. Italy's provision of aid is one of the highest in Europe, but the cost of these benefits has contributed to widening government budget deficits, and some Italian leaders have proposed cuts in social spending. These budget concerns are emphasized by the emergence of a growing elderly population. With a declining birthrate, Italy's population as a whole is shrinking, while the percentage of citizens over the age of 65 is growing. This shifting balance will pose a challenge to Italian policymakers and health-care providers in the years to come.

Cultural Life

One thing that Italy has rarely lacked is a thriving cultural life. From the poets and artists of the ancient Roman Empire and the Renaissance to modern-day filmmakers and sports figures, the country has developed a rich heritage that continues to grow. Although Italy, as a relatively young nation, may still be developing its image as a modern, sophisticated member of the international community, it is already recognized worldwide as a home of great art, entertainment, and culture.

▶ Religion

Roman Catholicism remains the dominant religion in Italy. More than 90 percent of the population belongs to the Catholic Church, which plays an important role in daily life. Italian Catholics often turn to their priests and other Church officials for advice and assistance. The Church operates hundreds of schools and hospitals, and Catholic charities provide an important source of aid for workers,

retirees, and the disabled. Church doctrine has had a strong influence on the laws of Italy and it remains a powerful social force in the early 2000s.

A treaty signed in 1929 established Vatican City as the world center for Roman Catholicism. Located entirely within the city of Rome, Vatican City is an independent city-state that is run by the Pope and is not subject to Italian rule.

In addition to Catholics, Italy also has a small population of Jews, most of whom live in Rome and Milan. Many Albanian and North African immigrants follow the Islamic faith, and there is also a small community of Italian Protestants.

Holidays and Festivals

Italians celebrate ten national holidays, including Liberation Day, which commemorates the Allied victory in Europe at the end of World War II, Labor Day, All Saints' Day, and New Year's Day. Nearly every village and city also has its own special festivals celebrating patron saints, historical events, or local harvests.

Easter, or la Pasqua, is the most important religious holiday for Italy's many Roman Catholics. In Rome thousands of people from all over the world crowd into the square in front of Saint Peter's Basilica to hear the Pope's Easter Sunday blessing, and Sicily is well known for its elaborate Easter processions and celebrations.

Christmas, or Natale, is another important holiday season in Italy. The season ends on January 6, also known as Epiphany. This is the usual day to exchange gifts in Italy, and la Befana, a character usually portrayed as an old woman with a broom, traditionally brings treats to good children and lumps of charcoal to naughty children.

Local festivals include the Palio—a traditional horse race in Siena—and the Regatta Storica—a gondola race on Venice's Grand Canal featuring gondoliers in historical dress. Around the country, food festivals called *sagre* celebrate the ripening and harvesting of local crops.

Literature

Italy's literary tradition can be traced to the time of the Roman Empire, when writers such as Catullus, Horace, and Virgil wrote in Latin. Literature in the Italian language began with the works of thirteenth-century lyric poets, who used local dialects instead of Latin to reach a wider audience. Dante Alighieri, a native of Florence and the author of *The Divine Comedy*, did much to establish the Florentine dialect as

This statue of Italian writer **Dante Alighieri** stands in Verona. He lived in Verona after he was exiled from his birthplace, Florence, for political reasons in 1302.

standard Italian among writers. Petrarch developed the poetic sonnet, and Giovanni Boccaccio collected one hundred tales in a book known as *The Decameron.*

Writers of the 1500s expanded their range of subjects. Written in an age of complex rivalries and political scheming, Niccolò Machiavelli's *The Prince* describes tactics for ambitious rulers. Baldassare Castiglione wrote *The Book of the Courtier* to guide his readers in proper manners at Italy's many aristocratic courts.

I Promessi Sposi (The Betrothed), a work by Alessandro Manzoni that was published during the Risorgimento movement in the nineteenth century, helped to spread the new standard Italian language to the country's readers. Gabriele D'Annunzio, a fervent Italian nationalist, wrote poems, plays, and novels during a career that bridged the nineteenth and twentieth centuries.

After World War II, Alberto Moravia penned

A ROMAN AFTERNOON

" [B]y the central fountain in Piazza Navona . . . there were numbers of children . . . chasing each other . . . ; and their mothers and sisters were sitting on the seats taking the air; and the swallows, rather like the children in the piazza, were chasing each other in the air, from one roof-top to another and round the obelisk."

—from *More Roman Tales* by Alberto Moravia

Rome's **Piazza Navona** remains a popular place for families and friends to meet and linger.

short stories and novels, including *The Conformist* and *The Woman of Rome*, that describe modern urban life. *The Leopard*, Giuseppe Tomasi di Lampedusa's tale of an old aristocratic family, reached a worldwide audience in translation. Italo Calvino wrote *The Baron in the Trees* and other imaginative novels about unusual people and occurrences. One of Italy's most well-known contemporary writers is Umberto Eco. His complex novels, such as *The Name of the Rose* and *The Island of the Day Before*, delve into history, language, and philosophy.

Music

Italy has been an important center of European music since the early Christian era. Pope Gregory I fostered the development of the Gregorian chant in the sixth century. By the eleventh century, Guido d'Arezzo, an Italian monk, had worked out a system of musical notation that later developed into modern music writing. During the Renaissance, new forms of secular music, such as the madrigal, arose in Italy.

In the 1600s, the Italian composer Claudio Monteverdi combined instrumental music, singing, and drama to create one of the world's first operas. Alessandro Scarlatti and Antonio Vivaldi also wrote music during the Italian Baroque era. In the 1700s, Italian composers developed the sonata, the dominant musical form in European music for the next two centuries.

Opera continued to stand out during the nineteenth and early twentieth centuries. Giuseppe Verdi wrote *Aïda, Otello,* and other masterpieces. Some of

Giuseppe Verdi's *Aïda* is a well known, popular Italian opera.

his music promoted Italian nationalism. Gioacchino Rossini's lively works include *The Barber of Seville* and *The Thieving Magpie.* Giacomo Puccini's *Madame Butterfly* remains one of the world's most popular operas. Gian Carlo Menotti, a contemporary composer, wrote *Amahl and the Night Visitors,* an opera often performed for children.

Although Italy has many venues for jazz, folk, rock, and other genres, the contemporary music scene is still dominated by classical instrumental works and operas. Each year music festivals take place throughout the country, the most renowned of which is the annual festival of music and drama in the hill town of Spoleto in central Italy.

Art

The art of the ancient Romans decorated private homes, public squares, religious buildings, amphitheaters, and palaces. Sculptors called on imagery from Greek and Roman mythology, while painters created portraits, landscapes, and still lifes. Roman architects designed massive temples, monumental arches, and public buildings, many of which remain intact. For example, the Pantheon, a meeting place built in the second century A.D. as a temple to the Roman gods, has survived in the center of Rome.

During the Renaissance period, Italian painters developed the science of perspective, which allowed artists to give more depth and realism to their works. Masaccio and Mantegna explored this new concept in their works, while Donatello brought lifelike emotions and poses to his sculptures. *La Gioconda (Mona Lisa)* and other masterful paintings of Leonardo da Vinci were only a small part of his pursuits, which also included hundreds of inventions, armaments, and engineering works.

Michelangelo's frescoes (paintings on wet plaster) in Rome are among the most celebrated works of art from the 1500s. His work on the ceiling of the Sistine Chapel in the Vatican still draws thousands of viewers every year. He was also noted for his powerful representations of biblical subjects in sculpture, including *David, Moses,* and the *Pietà.* The artist Raphael is

Always choosy about his materials, **Michelangelo** favored white marble from the town of Carrara for his statues. The region's prized stone is still quarried in modern times. *Moses,* one of Michelangelo's most famous statues, was one of his Carrara creations. However, repeated castings to copy it over the years have discolored the stone. In 2001 Italian restorers began the attempt to return it to its snowy hue.

well known for his frescoes, altarpieces, and portraits created during this period.

At the same time in Venice, the artists Titian, Tintoretto, and Giorgione were masters of oil painting. By 1600 the Baroque style of painting—with its realism, detailed scenes, and rich colors—was developing in Rome. Caravaggio was known for his realistic portrayal of religious figures as well as for his masterful handling of light and shadows. The Baroque sculptor Bernini decorated Roman palaces and churches.

Italian art declined in importance during later centuries, as new styles of painting were being developed in other parts of Europe. Giorgio De Chirico, a leading twentieth century Italian surrealist, depicted dreamlike landscapes and symbols in his canvases. Amedeo Modigliani, another twentieth-century painter, is known for his modern portraits.

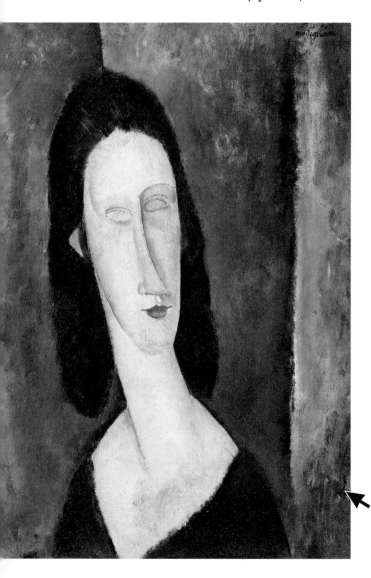

Italian painter Amadeo Modigliani had just met Jeanne Hebuterne when he painted her portrait, **Blue Eyes, Mrs. Hebuterne,** in 1917. She quickly became one of his favorite models.

Rome turned off the **Trevi Fountain** and draped its figures in black cloth to pay tribute to actor Marcello Mastroianni when he died in 1996. The fountain had been the site of one of Mastroianni's most famous scenes in the movie *La Dolce Vita.*

Film

Italians have been movie fans since film's beginnings. By the early 1900s, there were already several hundred movie theaters in Italy. In 1937, the famous studio complex Cinecittà was built outside of Rome and began production. Despite the crushing effects of World War II on the Italian economy and society, the movement of neorealism in the 1940s produced some of Italy's best films. Neorealist directors such as Roberto Rossellini strove to depict Italian life accurately, often filming on location in city streets and using amateurs in place of professional actors. *Ladri di Biciclette* (known in the United States as *The Bicycle Thief*) by director Vittorio De Sica is one of the classics of this time period.

In the 1960s, the Italian movie industry continued to gain international attention with director Federico Fellini's artistic, sometimes surreal films, including *La Dolce Vita (The Sweet Life),* and Sergio Leone's "spaghetti westerns" such as *The Good, the Bad and the Ugly.* Anna Magnani, Marcello Mastroianni, Sophia Loren, and other prominent Italian movie stars were famous around the world. Popular Italian films of the end of the twentieth century include *Cinema Paradiso, Il Postino (The Postman),* and Roberto Benigni's *La Vita È Bella (Life Is Beautiful).*

Loyal Italian **soccer fans** fill a stadium with their favorite team's colors.

Sports and Leisure

Italians enjoy a wide range of spectator and participant sports. The most popular professional sport is soccer. Led by international stars such as Roberto Baggio, Italian soccer players are among the world's best. Soccer is also enjoyed by nonprofessionals, who play from childhood in a variety of leagues. Other popular sports include basketball and volleyball.

Italian athletes have also excelled in Olympic competition. Downhill skier Alberto Tomba, popular at home and abroad for his confident, sometimes flashy style, carried home several gold and silver medals in

Skiers take on Mount Marmolada in northern Italy's Dolomites.

the 1980s and 1990s. The Italian runner Gelindo Bordin won the marathon in the 1988 games, and Italian teams took a total of thirty-four medals, thirteen of them gold, at the Sydney Olympics in 2000.

Italy's Alpine rivers provide fast-moving water for kayakers and canoeists, and ski resorts in the Alps and Apennines offer trails for downhill and cross-country skiers. Hikers enjoy a network of marked trails in the highlands. Sailors catch the wind off the Tyrrhenian seacoast and on the freshwater lakes of the north. Public tennis courts are common in Italian communities, and many golf courses have been built near the largest cities.

Food

Meals are an important part of daily life in Italy. The dinner table has traditionally been the central gathering place for families, who celebrate events such as weddings, birthdays, and holidays with long meals lasting well into the night. The modern workday has cut into leisure time, but many Italians still eat their largest meal in the afternoon, between a light breakfast of coffee and bread or a pastry and a small supper late in the evening.

Before a meal, cooks often serve a plate of appetizers, or antipasti. The plate may include prosciutto (ham), *formaggio* (cheese), vegetables, and bread and olive oil. A soup or pasta dish may be served next. Many different sauces are made for pasta, which also comes in dozens of shapes and sizes. Tomato sauces are an old favorite, as is *aglio e olio*, a simple sauce of garlic and olive oil. *Pasta alla carbonara* is noodles prepared with egg, parmesan cheese, and bacon, and pesto sauce is a mixture of olive oil, basil, garlic, and pine nuts.

Spaghetti is a delicious Italian pasta popular throughout the world. Italians have perfected the art of eating long noodles neatly. Visit vgsbooks.com for links to investigate the history and importance of food in Italian culture.

PASTA CON POMODORO

This simple recipe for pasta with tomatoes is best in the summer, when tomatoes and basil are ripe and delicious.

5 large tomatoes, peeled, seeded, and diced*

salt and pepper, to taste

1 pound spaghetti

½ cup olive oil

15 fresh basil leaves

1. Sprinkle tomatoes with salt and drain in a colander for about 30 minutes.
2. Bring a large pot of salted water to a boil. Add spaghetti, stir, and cook for 5 to 7 minutes, or until al dente (tender but firm). Drain spaghetti and transfer to a large bowl.
3. Add olive oil and tomatoes to spaghetti and toss well. Add salt and pepper to taste and leave to cool to room temperature.
4. Tear basil into small pieces and sprinkle over pasta. Mix well and serve.

Serves 4 to 6

*To peel and seed a tomato, bring a pot of water to boil. Cut a small "x" in the skin on the bottom of the tomato and carefully use a slotted spoon to add the tomato to the boiling water. Leave in water for 15 to 30 seconds. Remove with slotted spoon and run under cool water. The skin should be loose enough to peel off with your fingers or with a knife. Discard skin. Cut the tomato in half and cut out as many seeds as you can.

Italians take pride in many regional specialties. In Naples, the birthplace of pizza, restaurants prepare this popular dish with a variety of meats, vegetables, and sauces. Parma is known for ham and prepared meats, while Bologna, considered the country's culinary capital, is famous for tortellini (stuffed pasta) and Bolognese sauce. Polenta, a cornmeal dish, and risotto, a rice-based dish, are popular in Lombardy and the Veneto. A Venetian delicacy is pasta or polenta served in a special black sauce of squid ink. *Arancini* (deep-fried rice balls) and marzipan (a dessert delicacy made with almond paste) are Sicilian specialties. Italian wines are enjoyed at mealtime throughout the country. For dessert, many Italians look forward to fresh fruit, cakes, or rich, flavorful gelato (ice cream).

◉ Fashion and Design

Like so many endeavors in Italy, the fashion industry hit its stride on the world market after World War II. The nation's factories were already known for quality textiles, and Italy's artists and craftspeople had an excellent reputation for creativity and skill. Building on these strengths, Italian fashion designers introduced a distinctly new look in the 1950s and 1960s, emphasizing relaxed, easy elegance. Milan soon established itself as one of the fashion capitals of the world, alongside Paris, London, and New York. Italy continues to be known for high-quality clothes, shoes, and accessories, and designers and labels such as Versace, Armani, Gucci, Dolce e Gabbana, and Benetton are internationally recognized.

The same flair for style that made Italian fashion famous has also brought success to modern Italian design. Household objects of Italian production, from furniture to flatware, have gained great popularity and a wide market around the world.

A model debuts clothing by Italian designer Alviero Martini on the runway in a **Milan fashion show.**

THE ECONOMY

Until World War II, Italy's economy was based primarily on agriculture. The postwar years brought rapid economic growth as the country began to industrialize. After joining European trade associations, Italian industries expanded, and exports of manufactured goods soared. Turin and Milan became the principal manufacturing centers, while Genoa and Naples saw a rise in oceangoing freight traffic. By the end of the twentieth century, Italy had become one of southern Europe's most prosperous nations. Its estimated gross national product (GNP)—the value of goods and services produced by a country and its residents in a year—was more than $20,000 per person.

All regions of Italy did not share equally in the country's postwar prosperity, however. Well-paying factory jobs were plentiful in the north, while many southern Italians struggled in agriculture or in small, family-owned workshops. In 1950 the economic imbalance prompted the government to establish the Cassa per il Mezzogiorno (Southern Development Fund) to encourage industrial growth in

southern Italy. Although a few firms have relocated plants to this region, these plants tend to recruit management and skilled labor from the north, and southern Italy continues to lag behind the rest of the country in economic development and standard of living.

Other problems also persist in the twenty-first century. Social spending has caused rising budget deficits. In addition, the Italian state has a long history of controlling much of the economy through large, inefficient companies that dominate important manufacturing sectors, such as energy and chemical production. Privatization efforts to break up or to sell companies to private owners have made some progress, but the government must still deal with the debt incurred through years of running state-owned firms.

Manufacturing and Industry

The growth of Italy's manufacturing sector in the 1950s and 1960s made the country a leading economic power in Europe. With financial aid from the United States, Italian companies built hundreds of new factories, which sold their products to a growing European market. Italian automobiles, appliances, machinery, and other manufactured goods were shipped across the continent. Joining the European Coal and Steel Community in 1952 and the European Economic Community (forerunner of the European Union) in 1957 allowed Italy to greatly expand its exports. As one of the twelve member nations to adopt the euro in 2002, Italy continues to play an active role in the European Union.

Manufacturing contributes about 20 percent of Italy's gross domestic product (GDP)—the value of production solely within a country—and, combined with mining, employs more than 20 percent of the labor force. Northern Italy is still the home of most large industries, which produce automobiles, computers, and chemicals.

Machinery and automobiles continue to be some of the most important manufactured goods in the nation. Textiles, leather, and related goods made in Milan and surrounding cities make Italy an international center of the fashion industry. The chemical industry, which is also strong in Italy, manufactures rubber, fertilizer, plastics, and industrial chemicals such as sulfur and ammonium. The country also produces steel, appliances, and processed food.

Agriculture and Fishing

Once the mainstay of Italy's economy, agriculture plays only a minor role in modern Italy. Most Italian farms are family-owned operations with only small parcels of land. Crops cover more than one-third of the country's total land area. In hilly regions, farmers cut terraces into the hillsides to maximize the amount of level growing land.

The principal crops in Italy are sugar beets, corn, grapes, wheat, tomatoes, and olives. In the Po Valley, farmers grow corn and rice. Durum wheat (the main ingredient of pasta) thrives in Campania, Tuscany, and Emilia-Romagna. Umbria and Tuscany produce olive oil, while orange and almond groves dot the hills of southern Italy and Sicily. Tomato vines and orchards of cherry and apricot trees are common sights in Campania. Grapes flourish in Chianti, Asti, and Orvieto, which are world-famous wine-producing areas. In fact, wine is one of the country's most important agricultural exports.

Although not a major force in the farm economy, livestock raising in Italy includes beef and dairy cattle, pigs, goats, and chickens. Large herds of sheep graze in the highlands of Sardinia, and goats are common in southern Italy and Sicily. Farmers pasture buffalo in Tuscany and Campania for meat as well as for milk, which is used to make cheese.

Off the coast of Italy, **tuna fishing** is hard work, but it helps satisfy the domestic market for fresh fish.

The Italian fishing industry supplies the domestic market and draws on the waters of the Mediterranean Sea. Large catches of swordfish, tuna, anchovies, mussels, shrimp, squid, and octopi fill the nets of local fishing crews. Commercial fisheries also raise freshwater trout in inland lakes and rivers.

Energy

With few energy resources of its own, Italy depends on imports to supply more than 80 percent of its fuel needs. Most of these imports arrive from the Middle East and North Africa. A pipeline from Algeria, under the Mediterranean Sea, supplies more than 20 billion cubic meters (706 billion cubic feet) of natural gas to Italy each year. As a result, the economy is greatly dependent on stable world market prices for oil and natural gas.

Italian offshore oil refinery

Italian companies continue to search for oil and natural gas within the country. Small offshore facilities have been built in the Adriatic Sea and off the coasts of Calabria and Sicily. The country's largest natural gas fields are in the Po Valley.

In the late 1800s, a new hydroelectric plant was set up to supply Rome with power, making the Italian hydroelectric industry one of the oldest in Europe. Fast-moving rivers in the north continue to generate energy. The country has also developed coal, oil-burning, and gas-fired electricity plants, as well as nuclear power stations. In the late 1980s and early 1990s, however, safety concerns and public referenda (votes on proposals) forced the shutdown of Italy's existing nuclear plants and halted construction on new facilities.

Foreign Trade

Italy's position in the Mediterranean region has long made it a hub of international trade. For centuries Italy's cities exported textiles and other manufactured goods through busy ports such as Genoa and Naples on the Tyrrhenian coast and Venice and Bari on the Adriatic shoreline. After World War II, manufactured exports boosted the economy. At the beginning of the twenty-first century, Italy was running a small trade surplus, as tourism and the sale of exports were bringing in more money than the country was spending on imported goods.

Italy imports machinery, transportation equipment, chemicals, steel, and electronic goods. Italy buys much of its meat from abroad, and fuels make up a substantial portion of the value of the country's imports. Germany, France, Britain, the Netherlands, and the United States are the largest sources of imported goods.

Italy exports machinery (including automobiles), clothing and shoes, textiles and leather, food, and steel. Principal foreign customers for Italian products are Germany, France, the United States, Britain, and Spain.

SPANNING THE STRAIT

In 2001 the Italian government approved a funding plan for the Strait of Messina Bridge. If completed as planned, the bridge will take eleven years to build and will accommodate highway and railway traffic. At a length of 10,827 feet (3,300 m) from tower to tower, the bridge's central span will be the longest in the world.

Transportation and Tourism

Italy has well-developed road, rail, water, and air networks. After World War II, a massive program of road building linked the country's villages and cities. Southern regions—once served only by gravel and dirt roads—benefited the most from this program. A 4,000-mile (6,437-km) system of express highways (autostrade) runs between major urban centers, along with more than

Railroad tracks sweep along the Ligurian seacoast.

250,000 miles (402,325 km) of other roads that crisscross the country. Italian engineers also plan to build a bridge that will link the Italian mainland with Sicily.

Italy's railroad system dates to the late nineteenth century, when the newly unified Italian government made a large investment in modern rail lines. Travelers can journey from northern to southern Italy within a day on *rapido* and *espresso* routes. Slower *diretto* and *locale* trains stop at smaller towns and cross the Apennines, connecting Rome with the Adriatic coast. Bus lines serve remote villages.

Passenger ferries link the mainland with Sicily, Sardinia, and the Lipari Islands in the southern Tyrrhenian. International ferries run to Greece from Bari and Brindisi on the southeastern coast and from Sicily to the island of Malta to the south. Commercial cargo is transferred at Naples, Genoa, Palermo, and Bari.

Many of Italy's major cities have international airports. Leonardo da Vinci Airport, outside Rome, is the country's busiest and is a hub for flights linking Europe to the Middle East and Africa. Milan's Malpensa and Linate Airports are also busy centers. The national airline Alitalia operates both domestic and international routes.

Tourism has become one of the largest sectors of the Italian economy and is an essential source of income for many Italian businesses and workers. Millions of tourists arrive each year from all over the world to visit the country's cities, museums, historic sites, and recreational

The Leaning Tower of Pisa is one of the most famous tourist attractions in Italy.

areas. Venice, Rome, Florence, and Naples are all popular destinations, and even smaller towns such as Assisi, Perugia, Siena, and San Gimignano in the central highlands welcome their share of visitors.

Illegal Activities

Although its reputation and image have become legendary—and possibly exaggerated—through movies and stories, the Mafia is a very real presence in Italy. Originating in Sicily and dating back as far as the fourteenth or fifteenth century, the Mafia is an organization that engages in a wide variety of illegal activities. Its members are bound to each other by a familial loyalty and a code of silence and conduct known as *omertà*. Activities include drug trafficking (selling), arms dealing, and protection rackets (extorting money from businesses and individuals in return for protection from violence). In recent years, the Mafia's activity has broadened to include money laundering and investment in tourism, construction, and other areas that impact the Italian economy. In the 1990s, high-profile violence, including the assassination of two highly successful anti-Mafia judges in Palermo, along with the exposure of Mafia ties to politicians and public figures, led to a government crackdown on the organization.

Italy's anticrime and anticorruption campaign, which was most intense from 1992 to 1994, came to be known as the *mani pulite* (clean hands) operation.

Thousands of investigations and arrests were made, and in December of 2000 Italy was one of more than one hundred nations to sign a United Nations treaty to fight organized crime. However, the Mafia remains a force in Italian society.

Despite tightening law enforcement, prostitution, especially by immigrants, is another ongoing problem in Italy. Even more problematic is the trafficking of immigrant women and girls, most of them under twenty-five years of age, for the purposes of prostitution or other forced labor. Although exact figures are unavailable, the number of these women is estimated to be in the thousands.

◎ The Future

Despite Italy's many economic successes, some regions of Italy, especially in the south, remain underdeveloped. A wide gap between the rich and the poor exists and is worsened by unemployment and inflation. Italy's leaders have struggled to correct these problems, but a long string of unstable coalition governments has hampered reforms. Corruption and scandals have weakened the public's already shaky trust in the national government. And, despite Italy's role in a larger, international community—symbolized by its adoption of the euro—many Italians continue to feel more loyalty to their families, neighborhoods, and regions than to Italy or Europe as a whole.

As Italy entered the twenty-first century, it faced these ongoing issues as well as social problems, such as a growing elderly population, immigration, and crime. If the nation can come together to confront and overcome these challenges, it may also be able to achieve a lasting unity and prosperity and to stride ahead toward a bright, productive future.

Timeline

CA. 1200 B.C.	Etruscan settlers establish twelve city-states in Italy.
CA. 700 B.C.	Greeks settle southern Italy and Sicily, calling the area Magna Graecia.
CA. 510 B.C.	The Roman Senate overthrows last Etruscan king and founds the Roman Republic.
264-146 B.C.	Punic Wars
CA. 133-121 B.C.	Tiberius and Gaius Gracchus attempt to introduce reforms.
44 B.C.	Julius Caesar is assassinated.
CA. 25 B.C.–A.D. 180	Pax Romana (Roman Peace)
A.D. 64	A great fire destroys large parts of Rome.
79	Mount Vesuvius erupts, burying Pompeii and Herculaneum.
CA. 122	Construction begins on Hadrian's Wall in England.
330	Constantine establishes Constantinople as the Roman Empire's eastern capital.
CA. 476	The Western Roman Empire collapses.
CA. 568-774	The Germanic Lombards control Italy.
800	Pope Leo III crowns Charlemagne emperor.
962	Pope John XII crowns Otto I Holy Roman Emperor.
1130	The Normans establish a kingdom in Sicily.
1260s	The French take over Naples and Sicily under Charles of Anjou.
1282	Spanish Aragonese rulers take over Sicily.
1321	Dante finishes *The Divine Comedy*.
1436	The dome of il Duomo, the Florence cathedral, is completed.
1508-1512	Michelangelo paints the ceiling of the Sistine Chapel in Vatican City.
1600s	Peasant revolts break out in southern Italy.
1778	La Scala opera house opens in Milan.
1796	Napoleon's troops occupy northern Italy.

1815   Napoleon is defeated at Waterloo. Italy is divided among the victors, which include Spain and Austria.

1848   Rebellions in Europe inspire the Risorgimento in Italy.

1861   The unified Kingdom of Italy is founded.

1890   Italy begins the colonization of Ethiopia and Eritrea.

1908   A massive earthquake hits Sicily.

1911–1912   Italy conquers Libya.

1914–1918   World War I (Italy enters in 1915.)

1922   Benito Mussolini organizes a march on Rome and becomes the dictator of Italy.

1937   Cinecittà film studio opens.

1938   Enrico Fermi wins the Nobel Prize in physics for his study of neutrons.

1939–1945   World War II (Italy enters in 1940.)

1945   Mussolini is captured and executed.

1946   The Italian Republic is founded.

1957   Italy joins European Economic Community (EEC).

1960   The Olympics are held in Rome. Fellini's film *La Dolce Vita* is released.

1978   Former prime minister Aldo Moro is kidnapped and assassinated by the Red Brigades.

1982   Italy wins the World Cup soccer tournament.

1992   The assassination of anti-Mafia judges spurs a crackdown on crime.

1994   Silvio Berlusconi becomes prime minister, backed by the new Forza Italia party.

1997   Playwright Dario Fo wins the Nobel Prize for literature .

1999   Restoration of the Sistine Chapel frescoes is completed. The first female coach of an Italian professional men's soccer team is hired.

2001   Silvio Berlusconi is reelected as prime minister.

2002   Italy becomes one of twelve members of the European Union to begin using the euro, a new European currency.

COUNTRY NAME Repubblica Italiana (Italian Republic)

AREA 116,320 square miles (301,269 sq. km)

MAIN LANDFORMS Alps and Apennine Mountains; Mount Bianco, Mount Corno, and Mount Etna; Po Valley; main islands of Sicily and Sardinia; islands of Capri, Ischia, and Elba

HIGHEST POINT Mount Bianco, 15,771 feet (4,807 m) above sea level

LOWEST POINT Sea level

MAJOR RIVERS Po River, Arno River, Tiber River

ANIMALS Brown bears, chamois, roe deer, foxes, ibexes, moufflon sheep, wild boars

CAPITAL CITY Rome

OTHER MAJOR CITIES Milan, Naples, Florence, Venice, Palermo

OFFICIAL LANGUAGE Italian

MONETARY UNIT Euro. 100 cents = 1 euro

ITALIAN CURRENCY

The currency of the Italian Republic is the euro. One euro is comprised of one hundred cents. Between 1999 and 2001, the euro was adopted by Italy and eleven other member nations of the European Union (EU). Until 2002, the euro was only used for banking, credit card purchases, and other non-cash transactions. Coins and bills entered circulation in January 2002 and are issued by central banks and mints in participating EU nations, including Banca d'Italia (Bank of Italy). All nations share the same euro bills, illustrated with architectural designs, while each EU country created its own designs for the coin backs. All euro bills and coins can be freely used in any participating EU country. Italy's former currency, the lira, was completely removed from circulation on February 28, 2002.

Currency Fast Facts

Sometimes called *il tricolore* (the tricolor, or three-colored), Italy's national flag features three equally wide vertical stripes of green, white, and red. The basic design was first introduced in the late 1700s during Napoleon's reign. This design underwent many changes, including the placement of various coats of arms on the white field and, at times, the use of horizontal rather than vertical stripes. The modern form of the flag has been in use since the formation of the Italian Republic in 1946.

The Italian national anthem is titled "Fratelli d'Italia" (Brothers of Italy). Goffredo Mameli, a poet who lived during the Risorgimento and fought with Garibaldi's troops, wrote the words in 1847. Mameli's friend Michele Novaro composed the tune, and the song quickly became popular with patriots of the era. Following the hardships of World War II, "Fratelli d'Italia" enjoyed renewed popularity, and in 1946 it became the official national anthem of the Italian Republic.

An English translation of the first verse of "Fratelli d'Italia" follows:

> Brothers of Italy,
> Italy has arisen,
> With Scipio's helmet
> Binding her head.
> Where is Victory?
> Let her bow down,
> For God has made her
> The slave of Rome.
> Let us gather in legions,
> We are ready to die!
> Italy has called!

Discover what the melody of Italy's national anthem, "Fratelli d'Italia," sounds like. Go to vgsbooks.com for links.

ROBERTO BAGGIO (b. 1967) Baggio is one of the best soccer players in Italian history and an international star. Born to a large family in the small town of Caldogno, he loved soccer as a boy and joined his first club (professional team) when he was fifteen years old. Baggio has played in many Italian and European Cup tournaments and three World Cups.

JULIUS CAESAR (ca. 100–44 B.C.) Educated and ambitious, Roman-born Julius Caesar gained positions in Roman government as a young man. As a brilliant military leader, two of his most famous achievements were conquering Gaul (present-day France) and establishing Cleopatra as queen of Egypt. He introduced many reforms, including extended citizenship and a revised welfare system, but his power threatened fellow politicians and he was assassinated by members of the Senate.

DANTE ALIGHIERI (1265–1321) Dante was a poet and scholar born in Florence who wrote poetry, philosophy, and other works. He also served in the army and became involved in Florence's government. The subject of much of Dante's love poetry was a young woman named Beatrice. Although Dante saw Beatrice only twice, and although he and she both married other people, he remained devoted to her from afar. His greatest work was *The Divine Comedy*, an epic poem describing heaven, hell, and purgatory.

GRAZIA DELEDDA (1871–1936) Called Italy's best female novelist, in 1926 Deledda became the first Italian woman to win the Nobel Prize for literature. Born in a small Sardinian town, she started writing when she was very young and had her first story published when she was a teenager. Most of Deledda's work describes Sardinia and its people, and she is especially noted for her strong, vivid female characters. Her books include *Cosima* and *Reeds in the Wind*.

FEDERICO FELLINI (1920–1993) Born in the coastal resort town of Rimini, Fellini later lived in Rome. He worked sketching caricatures, writing for magazines, and scripting radio skits before becoming one of the writers for director Roberto Rossellini's film *Roma, Città Aperta (Open City)*. Fellini went on to become a world-renowned director, noted for intense and visually imaginative films such as *La Strada, La Dolce Vita*, and *8½*.

GALILEO GALILEI (1564–1642) Galileo was a mathematician and physicist from Pisa. He was particularly interested in the study of moving objects, from pendulums to planets. He made great strides in physics and astronomy, but his tendency to question long-held scientific and religious beliefs brought him into conflict with fellow scientists as well as with the Catholic Church.

GIUSEPPE GARIBALDI (1807–1882) Born in Nizza (in Liguria), Garibaldi became one of Italy's most-loved national heroes, fighting for freedom at home and in South America. He achieved his ultimate victory when he and his red-shirted troops conquered Sicily and southern Italy, helping to unify the country. His life was full of adventure and drama, from the tragic loss of his wife as she fought by his side in battle to an offer from Abraham Lincoln to command Union forces in the U.S. Civil War (1861–1865).

NATALIA GINZBURG (1916–1991) Ginzburg was an author known for her stories of family life. Born in Palermo, she later moved to Turin. Her father was a member of Italy's tiny Jewish minority, and her family was outspoken against Mussolini's Fascist regime. Ginzburg wrote novels, plays, and essays, and her literary career also included work as an editor and translator. While living in Rome, she served as a member of Parliament. Her works include *The Things We Used to Say* and *A Place to Live.*

LEONARDO DA VINCI (1452–1519) A classic Renaissance man, da Vinci excelled in fields across the arts and sciences. As a youth, he was the apprentice of an artist in Florence. He later opened his own studio and worked for a variety of prominent patrons including popes and kings. Two of his most famous works are the paintings *La Gioconda (Mona Lisa)* and *The Last Supper.* Da Vinci also explored sculpture, architecture, civil engineering, mechanics, and anatomy.

PRIMO LEVI (1919–1987) Born in Turin, Levi studied and worked in the field of chemistry. He also began writing poetry as a young man. Both a Jew and an antifascist, he was imprisoned in a concentration camp during World War II, and much of his postwar writing was about this experience. His works include *Survival in Auschwitz: The Nazi Assault on Humanity* and *The Periodic Table.* Levi wrote poetry, fiction, and memoirs.

RITA LEVI-MONTALCINI (b. 1909) Levi-Montalcini was born in Turin. Her mother was a painter and her father was a scientist and mathematician. Levi-Montalcini shared her father's interest in science, and she earned her college degree in medicine and surgery. As an Italian Jew in the 1930s, her career options were limited by Mussolini's discriminatory laws against Jews. Eventually she built a laboratory in her home where she could conduct research. During World War II, she offered medical treatment to refugees. After the war, she worked as a researcher and a professor, and in 1986 she and American Stanley Cohen shared the Nobel Prize in medicine for their studies of cell growth.

SOPHIA LOREN (b. 1934) Loren was born Sofia Scicolone in Rome. She grew up very poor, living in the suburbs of Naples with her single mother. Loren moved back to Rome as a teenager to pursue an acting career. She got her break when director Carlo Ponti—whom she would later marry—cast her in several movies. She changed her name to Sophia Loren in 1952 and went on to appear in more than seventy-five films, including *L'Oro di Napoli (Gold of Naples)* by director Vittorio De Sica, *The Pride and the Passion* with Frank Sinatra and Cary Grant, and *Pret-à-Porter* by director Robert Altman. Loren won a Best Actress Academy Award for *La Ciociara* (called *Two Women* in the United States) in 1961 and the Academy's Lifetime Achievement Award in 1990.

GUGLIELMO MARCONI (1874–1937) Marconi was born in Bologna and discovered his interest in science early in life. Studying independently, he was intrigued by radio waves and experimented at home with the transmission of radio signals. While working in Britain in 1901, he sent the first wireless message across the Atlantic Ocean, and in 1909 he won the Nobel Prize in physics. His discoveries made communication between ships and shore possible, leading to safer transatlantic travel.

MICHELANGELO (1475–1564) Michelangelo began his career as an apprentice to a painter in Florence. He produced great sculptures and paintings, from his monumental statue of *David* to his frescoes in the Sistine Chapel. The Sistine Chapel was a special challenge, as he had to paint the ceiling while lying on his back on scaffolding. Michelangelo also explored other creative fields, including poetry and architecture.

LUCIANO PAVAROTTI (b. 1935) Born to a baker in Modena, Pavarotti began singing in his local choir as a boy. He went on to study music and voice, and his opera debut was in Italian composer Puccini's *La Bohème* in 1961. Widely praised for his singing technique and his powerful voice, Pavarotti was soon starring in operas around the world, from Milan's la Scala to New York's Metropolitan Opera. He has made many popular recordings, and as one of the Three Tenors (along with Placido Domingo and José Carreras) he has helped bring opera to a wide audience. He also teaches classes and conducts music competitions.

GIUSEPPE VERDI (1813–1901) Born in a small northern village, Verdi studied music as a young boy. He was a brilliant composer whose works include the operas *Aïda*, *Otello*, and *La Traviata*. Verdi was also a devoted patriot, and his operas became beloved symbols of the Risorgimento. After Italy's unification, he was elected to Parliament, and when he died in Milan the streets filled with thousands of mourners.

FLORENCE Florence has been a top stop for culture and art since the Renaissance, and the Uffizi Gallery, housed in a sixteenth-century palace, showcases hundreds of Italian masterpieces. The city's cathedral, Santa Maria del Fiore (often simply called the Duomo), is a museum in itself, from the dome and massive bronze doors to the delicate mosaics and finely carved reliefs. For lighter diversions, visitors can stroll across the Ponte Vecchio (Old Bridge) or shop at an outdoor market.

MILAN As a prosperous, modern, northern city, Milan offers visitors stylish shopping and culture. The Galleria, a large glass-covered shopping arcade, is filled with restaurants and stores, and many top fashion designers have shops in an area of town known as the Quadrilatero d'Oro. The opera house la Scala is the place for world-class music, the ornate Gothic cathedral is a must-see for architectural enthusiasts, and Santa Maria delle Grazie Church houses da Vinci's *Last Supper.*

NAPLES Naples's historical occupants left a rich variety of monuments behind. The Royal Palace has a Spanish flair, while a thirteenth-century fortress built for Charles of Anjou shows French and Aragonese influences. The city's National Archeological Museum is one of the world's best and includes artifacts from Pompeii and Herculaneum, the ancient cities buried by the eruption of Mount Vesuvius.

PALERMO AND SICILY As Sicily's capital, Palermo has a long and colorful history. Its sunny streets and squares are crowded with churches and buildings displaying Islamic, Gothic, Norman, and Baroque architectural styles. Elsewhere in Sicily, Greek temples and theaters are reminders of an ancient past, and the active volcano Mount Etna looms on the island's eastern coast.

ROME Rome's sights are too many to list, but a few top attractions of the ancient city are the Forum, Colosseum, and Pantheon. Bernini's Fountain of the Rivers in Piazza Navona and Trevi Fountain are two of Rome's fabulous fountains. For a look at modern Roman architecture, visit EUR, a suburb built by Mussolini; for a bit of greenery, visit Palatine Hill or Villa Borghese; and for shopping, check out the Spanish Steps area or the Porta Portese Sunday flea market. And don't forget Vatican City, with its vast museum and Saint Peter's Basilica.

VENICE A unique city of winding canals and arching bridges, Venice's sights include early-morning fish markets, Saint Mark's Square— which floods at high tide—and the Rialto, a large bridge lined with shops. Saint Mark's Basilica and Santa Maria della Salute are two of the city's many churches. Art lovers can visit the Accademia museum, while history buffs can tour the Doge's Palace and the palace's prisons.

Baroque: a style of painting, architecture, music, and other creative expression, which first emerged in Italy in the late 1500s and influenced the arts through the 1600s. Baroque works tend to be ornate and dramatic.

coalition government: a government formed by multiple factions or parties. Coalition governments are usually forced to reach moderate decisions through consensus, and the governments tend to be unstable and ineffective.

Communism: a political and economic model based on communal, rather than private, property. In a Communist system, goods and the means of producing these goods are controlled by the government and distributed according to need.

European Economic Community (EEC): a multinational group formed after World War II with the goals of preserving peace among European countries and encouraging economic development and trade. The EEC was the main element of the European Union (EU), a group intended to strengthen economic, political, and social ties among the member nations.

fascism: a system of government that emphasizes the state or nation over the individual. Fascist governments are usually characterized by dictatorial leadership, limited economic and social freedoms, and the suppression of dissent.

gross domestic product (GDP): a measure of the total value of goods and services produced within a country in a certain amount of time (usually one year). A similar measurement is **gross national product (GNP).** GDP and GNP are often measured in terms of purchasing power parity (PPP). PPP converts values to "international dollars," making it possible to compare how much similar goods and services cost the residents of different countries.

nationalism: a philosophy or ideal valuing loyalty to one's own nation, preservation of national culture, and dedication to fulfilling the nation's needs

Red Brigades: an extreme leftist (liberal) Italian terrorist organization that gained international attention in the 1970s for bombings, murders, and other violent actions. The group's early goals were to weaken the Italian government and to inspire a revolution. In 1999 the group claimed responsibility for the assassination of Massimo D'Antona, a high-level government official.

Renaissance: a movement beginning in Italy between the 1200s and 1300s. Regarded as a transition between medieval and modern times, the Renaissance focused on a return to the classical ideals of ancient Greece and Rome. Its influence on art, philosophy, and science spread throughout Europe and lasted into the 1600s.

Roman Catholicism: a branch of Christianity headed by the Pope and based in Vatican City in Rome. Roman Catholicism is characterized by ceremony, ritual, and reverence for the Virgin Mary and saints as well as Jesus.

Socialism: a political and economic theory based on the idea of social rather than individual control of goods and production. The ideas of Socialism are very similar to those of Communism, but are generally broader and less extreme.

Belford, Ros, et. al. *Italy.* New York: Dorling Kindersley, 1996.
This illustrated travel guide provides historical and cultural details along with practical information for visitors to Italy.

Cable News Network. *CNN.com Europe.* 2001.
<http://europe.cnn.com> (May 7, 2002).
This site provides current events and breaking news about Italy, as well as a searchable archive of older articles.

Central Intelligence Agency. "Italy." *The World Factbook 2000.* 2000.
<http://www.cia.gov/cia/publications/factbook/geos/it.html> (May 7, 2002).
This site provides a brief overview of Italy's geography, demographics, government, economy, and military, complete with statistical information.

The Europa World Year Book 2000. **London: Europa Publications Limited, 2000.**
This annual publication covers Italy's recent history, economy, and government. It also provides statistics on population, employment, and trade.

Holmes, George, ed. *The Oxford History of Italy.* New York: Oxford University Press, 1997.
This title presents a detailed history of Italy from the Roman Empire through the 1990s, with sections highlighting politics, society, and culture.

"Italy." *Encyclopedia Britannica.* 2001.
<http://www.britannica.com> (May 7, 2002).
This site presents a detailed article covering Italy's geography, history, culture, social structure, and economy.

Lintner, Valerio. *A Traveller's History of Italy.* New York: Interlink Books, 1995.
This book surveys Italian history, with an emphasis on society and culture.

Moliterno, Gino, ed. *Encyclopedia of Contemporary Italian Culture.* New York: Routledge, 2000.
This title presents relatively detailed descriptions and explanations of elements of Italian society and culture, from motor scooters to women's rights.

"PRB 2001 World Population Data Sheet." *Population Reference Bureau (PRB).* 2001.
<http://www.prb.org> (May 7, 2002).
This annual statistics sheet provides data on Italy's population, birth and death rates, infant mortality rate, and other useful demographic information.

Shinn, Rinn S., ed. Foreign Area Studies, The American University. *Italy: A Country Study.* Washington, D.C.: U.S. Government Printing Office, 1987.
This title gives a moderately detailed overview of Italy's history, society, government, and economy.

Turner, Barry, ed. *The Statesman's Yearbook: The Politics, Cultures, and Economics of the World, 2001.* New York: Macmillan Press, 2000.
This resource provides concise information on Italian history, climate, government, economy, and culture, including relevant statistics.

Barghusen, Joan. *Daily Life in Ancient and Modern Rome.* **Minneapolis: Runestone Press, 1999.**
This title takes readers on a historical tour of Rome, from its founding to the present.

Bisignano, Alphonse. *Cooking the Italian Way.* **Minneapolis: Lerner Publications Company, 2002.**
This cultural cookbook presents recipes for a variety of authentic and traditional Italian dishes, including special foods for holidays and festivals.

Calvino, Italo. *Italian Folktales.* **Translated by George Martin. New York: Harcourt Brace Jovanovich, 1980. (Originally published in Italy in 1956.)**
This book is a collection of two hundred Italian folktales, selected and retold by Italo Calvino, a highly acclaimed Italian author.

Evans, Matthew, and Gabriella Cossi. *World Food: Italy.* **Oakland, CA: Lonely Planet Publications, 2000.**
This specialized travel guide takes a close look at eating in Italy and includes information about regional cooking, the cultural significance of food, and food festivals.

Foster, Leila Merrell. *Italy.* **San Diego, CA: Lucent Books, 1999.**
This book provides an overview of Italy's geography and history, along with modern life and culture.

Gentleman, David. *David Gentleman's Italy.* **London: Hodder and Stoughton, 1997.**
This book is an artist's colorful survey of Italian architecture and landscapes, accompanied by brief historical and cultural information.

Ginzburg, Natalia. *The Things We Used to Say.* **Translated by Judith Woolf. New York: Arcade Publishing, 1999. (Originally published in Italy in 1963.)**
This autobiographical novel describes a family's life in Italy, from Fascist prewar Italy to the aftermath of World War II.

McGinniss, Joe. *The Miracle of Castel di Sangro.* **Boston: Little, Brown and Company, 1999.**
This story of a small-town soccer team in the mountainous Abruzzo region provides a look at the cultural importance of Italy's national sport.

Murray, Willliam. *The Last Italian: Portrait of a People.* **New York: Prentice Hall, 1991.**
This series of essays offers glimpses of Italians and Italian life, from the daily routines of a Roman restaurant owner to the fast-paced business world of Milan.

O'Connor, Barbara. *Leonardo da Vinci: Renaissance Genius.* **Minneapolis: Carolrhoda Books, Inc., 2003.**
This biography discusses Leonardo's life, his art, and his inventions.

Further Reading and Websites

Scarre, Chris. *Chronicle of the Roman Emperors: The Reign-by-Reign Record of the Rulers of Imperial Rome.* **London: Thames and Hudson, 1995.**
This book provides a survey of the Roman Empire's rulers, from 31 B.C. to A.D. 476, supplemented by illustrations, maps, and time lines.

Sobel, Dava. *Galileo's Daughter: A Historical Memoir of Science, Faith, and Love.* **New York: Walker and Co., 1999.**
This biography of the Italian scientist Galileo, told partly through the letters of his daughter, offers a glimpse into his personal life, beliefs, and work.

Stone, Irving. *The Agony and the Ecstasy.* **New York: Doubleday, 1961.**
This highly researched novel tells the life story of Michelangelo, from childhood through death. The text is supplemented by a glossary and a list of Michelangelo's works.

Time-Life Books, eds. *Etruscans: Italy's Lovers of Life.* **Alexandria, VA: Time-Life Books, 1995.**
This title offers a description and history of the Etruscans and their lives in ancient Etruria. Photos and diagrams show examples of their homes, art, and personal possessions.

———— *Pompeii: The Vanished City.* **Alexandria, VA: Time-Life Books, 1992.**
This richly illustrated book looks at the ancient cities of Pompeii and Herculaneum and their preserved remains.

vgsbooks.com
Website: <http://www.vgsbooks.com>
Visit vgsbooks.com, the homepage of the Visual Geography Series®. You can get linked to all sorts of useful on-line information, including geographical, historical, demographic, cultural, and economic websites. The vgsbooks.com site is a great resource for late-breaking news and statistics.

Viola, Herman J., and Susan P. Viola. *Giuseppe Garibaldi.* **New York: Chelsea House, 1988.**
An informative biography of Garibaldi, a leading figure in the Risorgimento and one of Italy's national heroes.

Captions for photos appearing on the cover and chapter openers:

Cover: The Santa Maria del Fiore (Holy Mary of the Flower) cathedral is in Florence.

pp. 4–5 Giovanni Paolo Panini painted *Rome: The Interior of Saint Peter's* in the 1730s.

pp. 8–9 Tremezzo might be called a village of villas. It is one of many resort towns surrounding Lake Como, a popular tourist destination in alpine northern Italy.

pp. 38–39 Tourists and locals stroll the Piazza San Marco (Saint Mark's Square) in Venice.

pp. 46–47 The Pala d'Oro (Altar of Gold), an altarpiece adorned with more than three thousand precious stones and biblical icons inlaid in gold, may be viewed in the Basilica di San Marco (Basilica of Saint Mark) in Venice.

pp. 58–59 Genoa is Italy's main commercial port.

Photo Acknowledgments

The photographs in this book are reproduced with the permission of: © National Gallery Collection; By kind permission of the Trustees of the National Gallery, London/CORBIS, pp. 4-5; © Reuters NewMedia Inc./CORBIS, pp. 7; © Blaine Harrington III, pp. 8–9; © Sandro Vannini/CORBIS, p. 10; © Roger Rassmeyer/CORBIS, pp. 11; © Hulton-Deutsch Collection/CORBIS, pp. 33, 34; NASA, p. 12; © Scott Gilchrist, p. 14; © Galyn C. Hammond, pp. 15, 43; © Chuck Place/ PlaceStockPhoto.com, pp. 17, 25, 46-47, 48; © David Lees/CORBIS, p. 20; © Araldo de Luca/CORBIS, p. 22; © Archivo Iconografico, S.A./CORBIS, pp. 23, 28; © Chris Hellier/CORBIS, p. 24; © Musée du Louvre, Paris/SuperStock, p. 27; © Bettmann/CORBIS, pp. 30, 32; © Massimo Sciacca, pp. 35, 54 (top), 62; © Nicolas Sapieha/CORBIS, pp. 37; © Bob Krist/CORBIS, pp. 38–39; © David & Peter Turnley/CORBIS, p. 40; © Vince Streano/ CORBIS, p. 42; Association Montessori Internationale, p. 44; © Gino Russo, pp. 47, 49, 58–59, 61, 63, 64; © AFP/CORBIS, pp. 50, 57; © Philadelphia Museum of Art/CORBIS, p. 52; © W. Lynn Seldon, Jr., p. 53; © Vittoriano Rastelli/CORBIS, p. 54 (bottom); © Walter, Louisann Pietrowicz/September 8th Stock, p. 55; Todd Strand/IPS, p. 68.

Cover photo: © Gino Russo. Back cover photo: NASA.